THE GUIDES
OF THE
CHALET SCHOOL

JANE BERRY

Girls Gone By Publishers

Published by
Girls Gone By Publishers
4 Rock Terrace, Coleford, Bath, Somerset BA3 5NF

First published 2009
Chalet School characters © Girls Gone By Publishers
Text © Jane Berry 2009
Design and Layout © Girls Gone By Publishers 2009
Cover illustration © Girls Gone By Publishers 2009
Author photograph © James Scott 2009

The moral right of Jane Berry to be identified as the author of
this book has been asserted by her in accordance with the
Copyright, Designs and Patents Act 1988.

All rights reserved.
Without limiting the rights under copyright reserved above,
no part of this publication may be reproduced, stored in or
introduced into a retrieval system, or transmitted, in any form or by
any means (electronic, mechanical, photocopying, recording or
otherwise), without the prior written permission of the above
copyright owners and the above publisher of this book.

Girls Gone By Publishers, or any of their authors or contributors,
have no responsibility for the persistence of accuracy of URLs for
external or third-party internet websites referred to in this book, and
do not guarantee that any content on such websites is, or will
remain, accurate or appropriate.

Edited by Ruth Jolly
Cover design and adaptation by Ken Websdale
Typeset in England by AJF
Printed in England by CPI Antony Rowe

ISBN 978-1-84745-079-1

Simone was *still* leaking tears. (*page* 165)

THE AUTHOR

JANE BERRY was born in High Wycombe in 1979, and grew up in Beaconsfield and Norwich. She studied Renaissance and Modern European History at Warwick, during which time she spent three months living in Venice, and followed this with a Masters in Information Processing: Computers and the Man-Machine Interface (or, as she puts it, 'As much of a Computer Science degree as you can fit into a year') at York.

A voracious reader, she first encountered the Chalet School stories aged seven or eight when her mother tucked a copy of *The School at the Chalet* into her bed as a treat when she was being looked after by a babysitter. Juliet's abandonment by her parents caused a dreadful nightmare which she still remembers, and she only began to love the books when she was allowed into the High March School library a year later, where a full set of the original Armada paperbacks could be found. After this rocky start, she now has a full set of Chalet School stories in various editions.

When not reading, she is generally to be found knitting, sewing, organising the Brownies and Guides of 8th St Pancras, folk dancing and failing to get to the theatre quite as much as she might like.

She still hasn't been to the Achensee.

For my parents
GERALDINE AND RICHARD BERRY
You taught me how to read and write, how to
concentrate, how to persist, and you have
supported me every step of the way.

First Aid information given in this book is based on the Guiding syllabuses of the 1920s, and is not recommended as good practice in the present day.

CONTENTS

CHAPTER		PAGE
	Foreword	11
	Acknowledgements	12
I.	The Journey Begins	15
II.	A Budget of Letters	25
III.	Visitors: Expected and Otherwise	39
IV.	The First Day of Term	51
V.	Guides!	65
VI.	A Sunny Afternoon	78
VII.	Triumph and Disaster	91
VIII.	An Expedition	101
IX.	'Adieu, Sweet Lovely Nancy'	118
X.	Escapades	127
XI.	An Edict	142
XII.	A Spot of Morris	153
XIII.	Madame Pagnol	162
XIV.	A Long Night	173
XV.	Contemplation	180
XVI.	Exams …	190
XVII.	… and Tests	202
XVIII.	A Birthday Camp Fire	209
XIX.	The Folk Festival	220
XX.	Celebrations	231
	Afterword	240

FOREWORD

Around seven years ago, newly arrived in London and not knowing anyone, I decided that it might be fun to try writing a Chalet School book. I started by looking at Caroline German's excellent article 'The Chalet School: the Missing Books', and the title *The Guides of the Chalet School* rather appealed to me, so I embarked on my story, sitting on the sofa in a somewhat unprepossessing flat in Camden Town, escaping reality and settling firmly in the past, in a foreign country.

It wasn't long before I was pestering the archivists at Girlguiding UK's Commonwealth Headquarters in Buckingham Palace Road for information about British Guides in Foreign Countries. From there, it was a short step to deciding to re-involve myself in Guiding, gaining my Queen's Guide Award, and eventually becoming Brown Owl for 8th St Pancras Brownies, Joint Guider-in-Charge of 8th St Pancras Guides, and Queen's Guide Co-ordinator for London North West County.

Along the way, I have made a set of friends who have supported me through the bad times and had fun with me during the glad times. So many are also Chalet School fans and they have encouraged me to keep writing this book long after I might otherwise have given up.

With Girlguiding UK's Centenary Year in progress as this book is published; with half of all girls in the UK being involved in Guiding at one time or another in their lives; and with such fantastic opportunities on offer, in a unique girl-only space, what more can I say than 'Three cheers for the Guides!'

Jane Berry
2009

ACKNOWLEDGEMENTS

This book could not have happened without the support of many people. The Brownies, Guides and Rangers of Saint Pancras Division have provided real-life inspiration for the girls' behaviour, and an excellent introduction into the behaviour of 'Middles'.

The County of London North West sent me to Foxlease as part of an Arts weekend, giving me invaluable access to the log books of the period, and enabling me to go climbing across the roof myself. My original Guide Guider, Bridget Eade, in her role of Archivist for Norfolk County, gave me my initial interest in the History of Guides as part of my Baden-Powell Trefoil work. I would also like to thank Karen Stapley, Archivist, Girlguiding UK, for patiently answering queries regarding historical accuracy.

My friends Emily Beer, Kerri Brennan, Moira Collins, Heather Edmonds, Joanne Heritage, Lucy Honour and Kirsten Lowson listened to me bouncing ideas and helped me formulate them, while the members of the Girlsown Mailing List answered many of my random questions.

Helen Barber, in particular, helped me to crystallise 'the Aunts' and their families, while Caroline German helped me track down various bits of slang.

To Sam Skey I owe my introduction to New Esperance Morris, and I especially thank Fiona Anderson, Hilda Dedic, Zak Keir, Diane Moody and Mary-Jo Searle for their support and enthusiasm for the project and for the fun we had dancing. To Steve Harris, Matt Morris, Tom Richards, Jameson Wooders and other eCeilidh (English Ceilidh) dancing partners too numerous to list, thank you for making my feet fly as I researched and danced.

Thanks are also due to Stirling McGuire, pen historian, for information on the properties of 1920s ink.

My various flatmates have put up with my erratic behaviour while writing—thank you, Chris, Martin, Kristian, Sebastian and Claire, while Dafydd Biffen has looked after me and cooked for me, and supported me through the final drafts. My editor, Ruth Jolly, has done sterling work, and become a friend in the process.

I would like to thank James Scott for taking my photograph for the back cover of this book, and Michael Scott for the use of the Classics Department library at Cambridge University.

Finally, Emily Holbrook Treen has been my inspiration as a Guider, a writer, and a friend: I'm so sorry, Em, that you didn't get to hold this book.

Chapter I

THE JOURNEY BEGINS

Two girls stood next to a heap of cases and travelling rugs in the centre of the ticket hall at Victoria Station. There was nothing unusual in such a scene, yet something about this pair marked them out. The smaller of the two gesticulated animatedly as she chattered to her companion. Her lovely face was wreathed in smiles, and her dark curls bobbed as she nodded emphatically. The elder girl smiled down at her; and her pale, pointed face, with huge black eyes framed by straight, dark hair cut in page boy fashion, was full of life and character.

'Madge won't be long now, Robin: look! She's at the front of the queue. Better buck up and grab our cases,' remarked Joey Bettany.

She turned to do so, then gave an exclamation of dismay. A tall gentleman of choleric complexion, sporting a greying walrus moustache, had been hurrying to catch his train. In his haste, he completely failed to look where he was going, and tripped over a small attaché case belonging to the Robin.

'Oh, I am so ver' sorry,' the owner gasped, as the gentleman righted himself and glared at her. He was immensely tall and thin, and with his bushy eyebrows and fierce expression was a sufficiently daunting sight.

The little girl quaked.

'Youngsters today. No respect! Where is your mother, child? Why is she not looking after you?'

The Robin's mouth drooped, and tears welled in her eyes.

Her beloved Polish mother, who had taught her, and cared for her, and done everything for her, had died in decline just over a year earlier, and the little girl had been sent to the Chalet School, since her father was obliged to go on business to Leningrad—or Petrograd as it used to be called. Her Tante Marguérite, as she called Madge Bettany, was very kind; but she missed her mother dreadfully and felt her loss as keenly as ever.

Just at that moment, Miss Bettany arrived with the tickets and, smiling at the irate gentleman, apologised for leaving the girls. But even as she spoke, he caught sight of the Guide badge pinned to her lapel. He stiffened, and his face turned an alarming shade of purple.

'You are in charge of these girls?' he exclaimed loudly. 'I am surprised that their mother allows it, as you are certainly not old enough to take charge of anyone. I see you are a Girl Guide. Well. Harrumph!' and he stalked off, leaving Madge completely flabbergasted. Young she might be, but the Headmistress of the Chalet School had no qualms about her ability to care for her charges.

'Well!' ejaculated Joey. 'I do hope he's not on the same train as us. How dare he say that you're not old enough to look after us!' Jo was fuming, while the Robin still looked close to tears.

'It doesn't matter, Joey. But whatever did you do to make him so angry?'

'It was his own fault! He wasn't looking where he was going,' Joey replied, 'and he nearly fell over the Robin's attaché case. Then he started yelling and carrying on, and then you arrived.'

'Well, I don't suppose we shall see him again. Come along—platform two! Robin, have you your case? Joey, have you yours? And the rugs? Good. We shall have to hurry!' She smiled at the Robin. 'Come, *chérie*! It was not your fault. Bustle along!'

The Robin applied herself to scurrying as fast as her legs could carry her. In the hurry to catch the train, she forgot her troubles, and was soon back to her usual sunshiny self.

Alas for Jo! The gentleman with the moustache, as it turned out, was ensconced in the next compartment, fuming silently as he perused the contents of his newspaper. He too was travelling to Lyndhurst, where he had lived since his discharge from the Army. Accustomed to military life, Brigadier Harris mistrusted women in general and Girl Guides in particular.

His grievance against the Guides arose from an unfortunate incident a few years earlier. He carried on a harmless feud with his next-door neighbour, Commodore Bennett, late of the Royal Navy. Both exhibited vegetable marrows, and the competition between them was fierce. One year, a ball carelessly thrown by a group of Guides had smashed through the roof of the Brigadier's glasshouse, damaging the young plants, and Commodore Bennett had carried off the prize then and each successive year. Brigadier Harris was furious, and blamed the Guides; hence his behaviour to Madge. He harrumphed to himself, and shook his paper out.

Meanwhile the three girls settled themselves into their compartment, and Joey eagerly began to question her sister, who had spent much of the past two days interviewing candidates for the positions of English mistress and matron for the Chalet School. The school, which had been founded a year earlier to provide a home for Madge and the delicate Joey in the health-giving mountain air of the Austrian Tyrol, had grown to such an extent that Miss Bettany needed to take on extra staff. She had engaged a room in a hotel for the interviews, leaving the home of the aunt with whom they were staying early each morning and returning late in the evening, and Joey had had no opportunity to quiz her until this moment.

'Did you manage to get a matron? And another mistress? Will I like them? What are they like?'

Madge laughed. 'Yes, I believe I have a matron, Matron Wilson, who used to be at a boys' school. She is very friendly and capable, and comes from Scotland—she speaks with a delightful lilt. And a Miss Carthew will, I hope, join us for the English subjects.'

'Oh, but, Madge!' Joey interrupted. 'You aren't going to stop teaching us, are you?'

'Not altogether. I'll still teach you literature, but you'll have Miss Carthew for history and geography. I simply haven't time now to teach all the English subjects. Miss Carthew knows all the latest methods, and has excellent experience.'

Reassured, Joey turned to the other big question that was occupying her mind. 'What will it be like at Foxlease, Madge?'

Madge smiled. 'I'll know that when I've been there, silly! I'll write to you every day, shall I, and then you can find out all about it almost as fast as I do. Maynie says it's a wonderful place.' Miss Maynard, another of the mistresses at the Chalet School, lived in the New Forest not far from Foxlease, and Joey and the Robin were to stay with her during Madge's absence.

'And the main thing is, you're going to learn all about how to be a Guide Captain there, and then we'll open the School Company, and we'll all be Guides. I say,' Joey paused, struck by a sudden thought. 'Do you think the day girls, like Stéphanie, are going to be Guides too? It would be a shame if they couldn't join in the fun.' Stéphanie Pagnol had joined the school the term before, although she had not yet been able to take much of a part in out-of-school activities as her mother was very ill, and preferred to have her daughter close by. 'It would be so good if she could join in, and feel more a part of things. Guides does that, you know.'

Madge looked at her thoughtfully, recognising the truth of this statement.

'I'm sure we'll be able to work out some way for her to join in, and her cousin Aurélie, too. All the new Juniors will be boarders, so they'll join the Brownies with the Robin and the others, and Miss Durrant will be in charge of them, as she is a Brown Owl. I hope Miss Carthew is going to agree to be Tawny Owl.'

'What luck! Robin, did you hear? You've got a Brown Owl and a Tawny Owl already.'

The Robin looked puzzled, so Joey elaborated. 'Madge is to be in charge of the Guides, with all the Middles and Seniors, and you Juniors will have your own group of Brownies, and the lady in charge of Brownies is called a Brown Owl, and instead of a Lieutenant to help her, she has a Tawny Owl.'

The Robin was little the wiser for this somewhat incoherent explanation, but gathered that not only would the Juniors have their fun, but that they would have owls to help them.

'And do ze Brownies do what ze Guides do, Zoë?' she asked cautiously.

'Oh yes,' replied Joey. 'They earn badges too, and play lots of games, and learn to be helpful. You'll love that!' Her eyes sparkling, she settled back into her corner, and dug out her copy of *An Inland Voyage* ready for when she wanted to read.

She gazed eagerly out of the window for some time, enjoying the English countryside as it whisked past. Presently, growing bored, she asked her sister's permission to go for a walk down the train. She was full of fidgets after their visit to London—the Bettanys' aunts remembered only too well how ill Joey had been as a small child, and still tended to mollycoddle her unbearably. After so much enforced inactivity, she was keen to stretch her legs.

Since the train was a corridor one, and not crowded, Miss Bettany gave permission, and Joey walked first right down to the back and then up towards the engine. Her eyes widened at the sight of the Brigadier in his compartment as she went past, and she hurried on, but could not resist peeping in on her return. Then she gasped in horror at the unexpected scene. There, slumped on the floor of the compartment, lay Brigadier Harris. His face was pale and horribly contorted.

Immediately, Jo wrenched open the door of the compartment.

'Are you all right? You don't look well at all!'

'My chest!' he gasped. 'My chest!' The panic in his eyes was clear to see, and, as Joey bent towards him, he gripped her hand in fear. 'My chest!' he whispered again breathlessly.

Joey was momentarily at a loss. The Brigadier's skin was clammy to the touch, and she was unsure what to do next.

'Wait there. My sister is in the next compartment. She'll know what to do—she *always* does.' And, with this reassuring proclamation, she shot next door.

'Madge! Madge! Do come quickly! That man who fell over our cases at the station is in the next compartment, and oh, Madge, he looks simply *ghastly*!'

Miss Bettany laid down her book and leapt to her feet. In an instant she was in the next compartment, bent over the Brigadier, her keen eyes taking in the situation at a glance. Joey and the Robin stood just behind her, eyes wide with interest and fear.

'Don't worry! Let me help you into a more comfortable position. Do you have a travelling rug—no, don't try to speak, just look towards it.' Miss Bettany's voice was immediately reassuring.

Brigadier Harris looked up towards the luggage rack, where a rolled tartan blanket was neatly strapped to his case. Madge reached it down and tucked it round him expertly, then loosened his collar, and propped his feet up on the case.

'Now I'll send my young sister to find the guard, so he can arrange for you to be taken off the train at the next station, and for a doctor. Lie quietly. Are you comfortable now?'

The Brigadier nodded, the terrible fear gradually leaving his face as he realised that he was in safe hands.

'I shall be back directly.' Miss Bettany swiftly dispatched Joey to find the guard, and returned to the Brigadier's compartment with an extra rug to put under his head, the Robin following close behind her.

Miss Bettany sat down beside him, and began to talk in a calm, encouraging manner.

'Joey saw you as she was walking down the corridor. She's looking forward to becoming a Girl Guide, and she's very keen to practise observation. She saw immediately that you were ill, and only paused to make sure you were breathing before coming to find me.'

'And you're a Guide, too,' whispered the Brigadier.

'Yes. We're travelling to Winchester, in part so that I can go to Foxlease, the big training camp, to learn how to be a Guide Captain,' replied Miss Bettany. She knew that it was important to keep the Brigadier's attention engaged while they waited for help. 'I am the Headmistress of a school in the Austrian Tyrol, the Chalet School, and we'll be starting the first English Guide company in Austria this term. I expect we'll call ourselves 1st Tiern See Guides.' She proffered a cup of tea from the flask she had brought from the other compartment. 'Here. Drink this. You've had a shock.' Slipping an arm under his shoulders, she encouraged him to sit up enough to take the drink.

The Brigadier nodded. The pain in his chest was easing, and he appreciated the quiet, competent way Miss Bettany was looking after him. He began to wonder whether he had not been a bit hasty in his judgment of the Guides who had damaged his marrows. After all, they had tried to make amends and had offered to repair the glasshouse.

'Thank you,' he whispered. He sipped at the tea, and began to feel a little more himself.

'Hush,' replied Miss Bettany quietly. 'Save your strength for when we reach the station. Yes, Joey?' Her younger sister had opened the door of the compartment and poked her tousled head round.

'The guard is on his way, and he says we'll be at the next station very shortly.' Joey spoke breathlessly after her hasty search of the train. 'I do hope you're feeling better,' she continued, her pity aroused by the sight of the Brigadier bundled up in a blanket. 'My sister's a topping nurse,' she added; 'she's looked after me heaps of times,' and so saying, she took the Robin by the hand and led her back to the neighbouring compartment.

'Your sister?' inquired the Brigadier. He was feeling somewhat better, and more able to take an interest in his surroundings. Madge and Joey Bettany did not, at first glance, resemble each other. Where Joey's complexion was sallow, and her dark hair straight, her elder sister combined curling dark brown hair and deep brown eyes with a wonderfully fair Saxon skin.

'Yes, our parents died when she was just a baby. I have looked after her ever since. She's given us some very worrying times. Now, hush!' Madge said firmly. 'Drink some more tea; I think we are almost there.'

Indeed, the train was slowing as it began the pull into the station. Soon the Brigadier was helped from the carriage and into a small room adjoining the Station Master's office, there to await the doctor. He smiled weakly in farewell to Miss Bettany, who rejoined the others, and the train pulled out of the station once more.

'Golly,' remarked Joey. 'That was unexpected! It was a bit like something in a book—oh, Madge, just imagine if he'd tapped out the SOS like the lady in *Peg's Patrol* did when she was tied up by robbers in her compartment! Robbers, too! That would have been simply *thrilling*!'

'I think I'm quite glad that we didn't have that sort of thrill,' Miss Bettany replied. 'Finding him so ill was quite enough for one trip!'

'I s'pose so.' Joey was a little crestfallen. 'Still, he looked much better when you came to help him. That was awfully clever of you, knowing exactly what to do.'

'And it was very clever of you to notice that he wasn't well, and come and find me, too,' Miss Bettany said with a warm smile at her sister. 'You did very well!'

Heartened by her sister's words, Joey settled back on her seat, and buried herself in her book as the journey continued.

Before long they were arriving at Winchester, where Miss Maynard was waiting on the platform. The two grown-ups greeted each other warmly, and for a few minutes they all talked at once. But the time soon came for the little party to break up amid a flurry of hugs and good-bye kisses. Madge was borne away to the great Guiders' training camp, and the rest of the party caught a local train to Lyndhurst village, where the Maynards' big car was waiting to whisk them along the remaining seven miles of their journey. The Robin was tucked safely in on the back seat and soon nodded off to the purr of the engine. Joey, however, made great efforts to stay awake, looking out of the windows of the car in an effort to catch sight of the famous New Forest ponies.

'Bed for you, the moment we arrive, young lady!' remarked Miss Maynard, noticing that Joey was starting to look 'all eyes', though she knew better than to fuss her about it.

'Oh, must I, Maynie?' replied Jo, who never would own to feeling weary. 'I'm not really that tired, and I do so want to see the house.'

'You will see it in the morning. You'll have a much better time tomorrow if you go to sleep quickly tonight.'

The Squire and Mrs Maynard were waiting to greet them when they arrived at the house. Joey, more tired than she would admit, stumbled over her greetings, and the Robin was so fast asleep that Mr Maynard scooped her up in his arms and carried her up to her room. Joey and Miss Maynard followed; and while the latter put the Robin to bed, Joey partook of hot milk and biscuits before she too slept.

Chapter II

A Budget of Letters

THE next day dawned bright and sunny, a perfect spring morning. Joey and the Robin found themselves in a dainty room which had a prettily patterned wallpaper covered in roses in two shades of pink, with plain pale pink curtains and deep pink eiderdowns to match.

'*Mais où suis-je, Zoë?*' asked the Robin in the French which still came to her more easily than English.

'*T'es à Pretty Maids, la maison de Maynie et ses parents.* But you must try to speak English, because I don't know how much French Maynie's parents know. Shall we get up?' replied Joey, sliding out of bed and putting on her slippers and dressing gown. 'Oh, isn't it *wonderful* to be out of London.'

The two girls were quickly ready, and Joey was putting the final gloss on her dark hair when the maid came to call them for breakfast. Mr Maynard was a stickler for punctuality. He said that it was not fair to keep the servants waiting, and it was a discourtesy to the cook not to eat her meals when they were piping hot and at their best; particularly when she had prepared a magnificent breakfast in honour of their guests, with porridge, scrambled eggs, bacon, and kidneys (Mr Maynard's especial weakness) on the sideboard. There was home-made marmalade and raspberry jam to go with the toast, and altogether it was a great contrast to the girls' usual breakfast. The Robin had never seen anything quite like it, and insisted on having 'a tiny bit of *everything*' to try.

'We don't normally have quite such a spread with just the two of us, but we thought we'd celebrate your arrival,' explained Mrs Maynard, 'especially since you two didn't have much supper last night.'

'Thank you, Mrs Maynard,' replied Jo, hastily swallowing a mouthful of bacon. 'This is a great treat. Usually we just have bread rolls and bowls of milky coffee.'

Their hostess laughed and turned to her daughter. 'Now, my dear,' she said, 'what are your plans? Jack will be arriving some time this afternoon, and Lydia and Rolf will be coming down on Monday to join us for a week. Bob can't be with us, because he is needed in Aldershot.' Jack and Bob were 'Maynie's' brothers, and she saw them all too seldom now that she lived in Austria.

At her mother's pronouncement Miss Maynard grimaced, since her nephew Rolf, son of Bob and Lydia and a year or so younger than Joey, was a spoilt, disagreeable young man, whose mother gave in to his every whim and blamed everyone but herself for her son's bad behaviour. 'Maynie' had very little time for Rolf, but she held his father, her eldest brother, dear, and beyond this slight frown, there was no change in her demeanour.

'Rolf knows all the nooks and crannies in the area, Jo, dear, and I'm sure he'll show you all the places that we grown-ups have forgotten about!' continued Mrs Maynard.

Miss Maynard doubted whether the young man would be quite so forthcoming about his secret places, but she kept her doubts to herself, since she wanted Joey and the Robin to meet him without prejudice.

'When will Miss Bettany be arriving?' inquired Mr Maynard.

'She's coming on Monday,' replied Joey, taking his question to herself. 'The training course only lasts a week. Why d'you ask?' she inquired with interest.

Mr Maynard chuckled inwardly. He was used to young people,

having brought up three of his own, and understood that Joey, accustomed to be on equal terms with her grown-up brother and sister, did not mean to be rude.

'I thought we might have an Easter Egg hunt when she's here, and roll them down the hill when we've found them. We did it with the local children at Easter.'

'An Easter Egg hunt! How ripping!' cried Joey.

The Robin, too, could barely contain her excitement, and beamed all round the table, although it must be confessed that she was not entirely sure what an 'Easter Egg hunt' was, or why one should want to roll down hills.

'Is it a ver' tall hill that we roll down? Me, I am not sure that I would be able to.'

At the thought of little Mrs Maynard, a bright-eyed lady in her sixties, rolling down a hill, followed by her husband, Joey was unable to contain her laughter. She spluttered into her tea, nearly choked, and had to be given several thumps on her back before she fully recovered her breath. The Robin looked her concern, but Mrs Maynard leaned over and patted her hand.

'Oh, Robin!' she smiled. 'We do not go rolling down the hill; it is the eggs that roll. It's a very ancient custom, which we thought you would enjoy.'

Reassured by this statement, the Robin returned happily to her milk.

After breakfast, the two girls retired to their room to discuss the day ahead. It had been decided that they would spend the morning exploring Pretty Maids and its gardens with Miss Maynard, after which she would depart for the station to collect her brother, while Joey and the Robin would spend their afternoon with Mrs Maynard. An old cricket set of Jack's had been located, and the three amused themselves with 'French' cricket for an hour or so, before the novelty of the game waned, and they moved on to clock golf, an almost permanent fixture on Pretty Maids' lawns during the summer months. Occasionally it was changed for croquet, but Mrs Maynard found croquet mallets quite a handful herself, being less than five feet tall, and knew that Joey would struggle, and the Robin be entirely unable to manage them. Clock golf was much easier, as there was an old set of miniature golf clubs in the summerhouse that had belonged to the Maynard children.

Toward four o'clock, and for the second time in as many days, the big car rolled down the driveway to the house. Jack Maynard leapt out almost before it had come to a complete halt, and hailed his mother, before running across the grass to envelop her in a bear hug. His sister followed at a more sedate pace, while Joey and the Robin, caught up in the general happiness, but aware that it would not be right to interrupt a reunion between mother and son, hung round the edges of the party. They did not have long to wait. Miss Maynard was quick to introduce them.

'Jack, this is Joey,' drawing her forward, 'and the Robin, whom I told you about on the way from the station. Joey and Robin, this is my brother Jack.'

Joey stuck out her hand, and politely inquired, 'How do you do?'

Jack shook her hand with equal solemnity, before his face broke into a great grin. After the fun of the afternoon, her hair stood out at all angles like a golliwog's, and there was a huge grass stain on her skirt where she had fallen while fielding a particularly strong hit by Mrs Maynard; her appearance was decidedly at odds with her formal manner, and this tickled his sense of humour. The Robin was in a far better state, although her curls were somewhat rumpled.

A gong sounded in the house, and they hastened inside to wash hands and faces (and in Joey's case reduce her hair to something less startling in nature) before the hot muffins that Jack knew would be ready to meet him on his return got cold.

*

From Joey Bettany at Pretty Maids to Madge Bettany at Foxlease

Dear Madge,

We are having simply the most scrummy time! (Yes, I know that's slang, but it's not term time! And at least I can tell when I'm doing it.) Mr and Mrs Maynard have been so very welcoming to us (it does seem funny to hear the servants call him 'the Squire', as though he's a character in a Victorian novel!), and it's such a lovely change to be out of London. It's not that I don't want to see the aunts, but they do *fuss* so! Of course, George is a good sort, and my other Heritage cousins aren't so bad—and Aunt Josie is a dear—but give me the country every time. And I don't understand how Aunt Daph *can* pretend to enjoy my piano playing!

We had a great time on Saturday. First we played French cricket, and then clock golf, and Maynie's brother Mr Jack Maynard came home from university. He's studying to be a doctor, but he doesn't fuss over me at all, and he's great fun. He's an Oxford Rowing Blue, and has promised to take us out on the lake if it's warm enough: although I doubt he'll let us row ourselves. He doesn't seem too keen on that idea. I'm simply aching to try rowing again, and see if I can remember all that we learnt last summer. Do you think, Madge, that we'll be able to do our Boatswain's badges if we can get in enough rowing when we're back at school? Or perhaps during the summer holidays, when we can spend days at a time in the boats again?

It's heavenly to be here, and we do such a lot during the day. The Robin is very happy to go to bed early, but I sit up later and read. Maynie thinks that Rolf, when he arrives, will do the same. It'll be odd to spend time with just one boy, not like having the cousins at all. I hope Rolf is as much fun as George.

How much have you learnt at Foxlease? Are you brilliant at knots yet, and can you track a horse a hundred miles? I'm ploughing on with all the knots and the Robin is doing her best with learning to knot her Brownie tie. She has become very good at plaiting Maynie's hair for her, and Maynie says that she's a great help in the morning! I can tie the clove-hitch, and the sheet-bend, and a bowline, and I'm sure that even if I'm not allowed to row, I'll be able to tie the boat up firmly. Oh Madge, do please say that I can try rowing? Maynie's brother *might* let me if I've got your blessing. Please do!

It's strange not having you here, but I know it's only for a few more days, and then you'll come back as a fully fledged Guide Captain, and we'll be even more ready to start the company at school. 1st Tiern See Guides, doesn't it sound *grand*? There's something very special about being the first, don't you think? Will we be the first Guide company that's a mixture of English and non-English? Or were there companies like that in India? I wish I could remember India, but I was much too small when we left. I can't remember it at all—only things that you and Dick have told me, and then I imagine very hard.

Oh, do write soon, and tell me what you've been doing. I can't wait for Monday, when you'll be back: we're going to have an Easter Egg hunt, Mr Maynard says, and roll the eggs down the hill. The Robin thought that we might be rolling down the hill with the eggs, which was very funny. She sends her love and kisses.

With love,
        Joey

From the Robin at Pretty Maids, to Tante Marguérite at Foxlease

Chère Tante Marguérite,
Tu me manques, et je t'envoie beaucoup de bises! Joey and I have had lots of fun, and I hope you have lots of fun too.
Love from
        Robin
        xxxxxxx

From Madge Bettany at Foxlease to Joey Bettany at Pretty Maids

Dearest Jo,

I know that you'll be bursting for an answer about boating, so I shall answer that first. Yes, of course you have my permission to row, as long as you have a grown-up with you. Remember, though, that you are a guest, so the final decision as to whether you are allowed to row lies with the person who is taking you out. If Maynie's brother is more comfortable rowing you than vice versa, you must respect his wishes! I am sure she has told him all about your exploits at school, and he will form his own judgment on the subject.

I have been doing such a lot here—every hour has been filled with bustle, and I'm writing this during our rest hour. Oh, Joey dearest, I do hope that you can come and camp at Foxlease one day. It really is a beautiful place.

We arrived on Friday, with the flowers beginning to bloom in welcome, and settled into the drawing room to be told what would happen next. It's a wonderful drawing room, all 'Strawberry Hill' panels, painted white and gold: a very special place. We've been divided into patrols: I'm a Chiffchaff; the others are Rooks,

Chaffinches and Greenfinches. I'm sharing a room with a girl from Canada called Alison Leach, and I've learnt such a lot from her. The Canadians come over to Foxlease to learn to train their own Guide leaders, and they've been practising on us.

We've started each morning with Drill, then talks on 'The Patrol System', or 'Company Management', or 'The Psychology of the Girl of Guide or Brownie Age', and then practical work such as signalling—I'm ashamed to say that it took me quite a while to remember all I learned when I was a Guide—as well as taking Heights, Weights and Distances: all those things which are part of your Second Class tests. We've been going on rambles (on our first ramble, the Chaffinches managed to find seventy different specimens of flowers and grasses, which is apparently a record!), and had country dancing in the Barn, company meeting, then supper and a camp fire. We have the luxury of a camp fire every night, although we have to light it using just two matches, the same as for the Second Class badge. I managed fine, but I did wonder if I would be able to get the fire lit before the match went out, as it was rather a windy day. Tomorrow night, each patrol has to perform a song or a stunt, and we've been racking our brains to think of something good.

I've particularly enjoyed the lectures we've had. You know how I once hankered to go to university: of course, that couldn't be, and I honestly wouldn't give up the Chalet School for the world now. Well, these lectures have given me a taste of what university would have been like. I'm learning some of the things that I might have learnt there, and it's absolutely fascinating. I've been given plenty of ideas for further reading, and I'm sure I'll be far better equipped to guess what you young monkeys are up to!

(Next Day)

Joey, I'm sorry: my letter was interrupted yesterday, and now

I can't possibly post it without telling you why.

Just as I'd finished writing that last sentence, there was a knock on the door, and one of the other Chiffchaffs burst into the room, yelling about a female inmate who had escaped from Lyndhurst Asylum! There was only one warder to chase her, so naturally we had to help. All we were told was that she had a mania for cutting people's hair—don't worry. Mine is still firmly attached!

We tracked her through the woods, picking up hairpins and ribbons as we went, and when we got to the other side, there was the warder, or so we thought, lying still and motionless on the ground. There was nothing we could do for the poor fellow, but a glisten of hair oil on the leaves beside him suggested that the lunatic might have had something to do with it. With fear beating in our hearts, we followed the trail back into the woods. Further in, there were mirrors and combs: and we were very much in need of these ourselves by this point. However, there was a lunatic to catch, so we continued onwards.

The leaves rustled overhead, and the birds seemed all at once to be very quiet indeed. We crept on. Suddenly, we heard an eldritch cackle, and there was the lunatic, hidden away in one of the shelters we'd built that morning, laughing demonically! And, can you guess who she was, Joey? None other than the Chiffchaff Patrol Leader for yesterday (we take it in turns to be Patrol Leader): and the warder was another Chiffchaff!

I shall stop here, so that you have a letter to read tomorrow. My love to you and to the Robin. Her note was very sweet, and I am enclosing a picture postcard of Foxlease for her. Be good, and enjoy yourselves.

With love to you both,

Madge

*From Madge Bettany at Foxlease to the Robin at
Pretty Maids*

Ma chère petite Robin,

I am glad that you are enjoying yourself at Pretty Maids. Thank you for all your kisses! I am having lots of fun at Foxlease. I hope you like this postcard—you can almost see the room I am staying in. I have drawn an arrow pointing to where it is.

Je t'embrasse,
        Tante Marguérite

*From Miss Maynard at Pretty Maids to Miss Bettany
at Foxlease*

Dear Madame,

I am so very glad that you're enjoying yourself, and that you've found Agnes Maynard in the log books there: I wondered if you would see her name. She's a distant cousin who founded one of the first Guide companies in London, so she's been Guiding for many years.

Joey and the Robin are in excellent fettle, if a little tired: Pretty Maids is in a hollow, and I did wonder whether it would suit them so well as the Tiern See. However, they are both going to bed at a sensible hour—Mother has seen to that—and they are eating well, so I don't think that there is much to worry about. Joey, in particular, has been 'making up for lost time', as she puts it, and haring around the gardens during her waking hours. She is keen to know the history of the house, and adores finding all the different nooks and crannies. She tells me that she felt extremely cooped up in London: evidently, she is a country girl at heart!

We're awaiting your arrival with impatience. You'll arrive just after my sister-in-law Lydia, Bob's wife, and their son Rolf.

I've not said much about Rolf to the girls, as I want them to meet on equal terms, but really, Madame, I am sure you will never come across quite such a spoilt child. He was very ill when he was small, and I think this has something to do with it: not everything, for Joey was ill too, from what you've told me, and she's a grand kid. Of course, Bob, being nearly eleven years older than I, remembers how we lost my sister Dorothy as a baby, and then how our brothers Steve and Charlie died of typhoid three years later, when Jack and I were very small. Mother and Father never really got over it, and Bob was quite old enough to understand: so I think he has been more protective of Rolf than he should have been, and Lydia's followed suit.

I hope you are learning all sorts of new tips to help us with the opening of the 1st Tiern See. The training courses I have been on at Foxlease were absolutely excellent. Have you worked out that you can get on to the roof from the Quiet Room, at the front of the house? It's worth peeping over the parapet to look at the view. (I remember one Guide being very adventurous and crossing the roof. She got stuck up there, and had to escape back down via one of the trainers' rooms, which was really rather hair-raising for her!) I wish we were all there to join in one of your camp fires: I look forward to our first one in the Tyrol.

Yours affectionately,
           Mollie Maynard

From Miss Bettany at Foxlease to Miss Maynard at Pretty Maids

Dear Mollie,

Oh, we have been getting up to plenty of high jinks here: if not climbing up on the roof, we have been chasing escaped lunatics—Joey will be able to tell you all about that—and trying to drill some of the most mischievous Guides I have met.

We began with a talk about the different types of drill, and our instructor told us, quoting B-P, that 'growing girls are very apt to slouch'. Some of the Guides of 3rd Lyndhurst, who had been drafted in for us to practise upon, straightened up perceptibly, and tried their best to look as though they had been standing very straight all along! They did a very good demonstration under our instructor's directions, even performing 'Empress Eugénie's Chair': I'd like to see some of our Middles managing to get into a circle and all sit down on each other's laps without falling over. I'm not sure they could!

The problems came when they were handed over to us for practising. They'd been told that there were going to be a lot of captains present, and that they should obey all of them. The mischievous little monkeys did just that! They obeyed every single order that they could hear. So one patrol was performing 'about turn' without stopping, another patrol didn't seem to be able to halt, and a third couldn't seem to keep marching for more than two steps at a time. It was chaotic, to say the least!

I finally put a stop to it by telling the patrol I was in charge of to obey just my orders and those of the girl I was working with, and that solved it. I can just imagine them plotting out what they were going to do; and I am sure they must get fed up with coming to Foxlease to be drilled—although I must say that they are a very smart company when they do follow orders correctly! I have learnt a simply enormous amount, and I do wonder if I shall be able to remember it all when it comes to running our own company.

I am a little concerned by what you have told me about Rolf, but I am sure that Joey is more than capable of holding her own against him, and of looking after the Robin while she's at it! Perhaps as he becomes older he will settle down.

  Yours affectionately,   Madge Bettany

*From Mrs Maynard at Pretty Maids to her daughter-in-law
Lydia Maynard in Aldershot*

My dear Lydia,

We are looking forward to your arrival after the weekend, although it is such a shame that Bob is unable to join us. Jack is here already, as well as Mollie, and two of Mollie's pupils—Joey Bettany and Robin Humphries. Joey's elder sister Madge, who runs the school, will arrive on Monday, as she is up at Foxlease at the moment. Joey's a little older than Rolf, and the Robin is a dear little creature of seven, who is being brought up as Joey's younger sister.

We are planning to have an Easter Egg hunt for the children, and I am sure Rolf will enjoy this; however, both Jack and Father have made it quite clear that if Rolf behaves as badly as he did on his last visit, he won't be allowed to join in the fun, and that would be a great pity. I'm sure he has matured since last time, and there won't be any need for him to be excluded, but at the same time, it is only fair to let you know.

With love from us both,

Mother

*From Lydia Maynard in Aldershot to Mrs Maynard at
Pretty Maids*

Dear Mother,

Rolfie and I are very much looking forward to our visit to Pretty Maids, and he has promised to be on his very best behaviour. Bob had a very serious talk with Rolf before he left on manoeuvres, and he has really been very much improved since then. He has been threatened with all sorts of dire, and, I am sure, entirely unnecessary punishments. Really, I have no doubt that he will be perfectly behaved! Bob sends his apologies, but—the Army is the Army, and duty calls.

I am very much looking forward to being at Pretty Maids, away from the brouhaha of Aldershot. I sent our trunks on ahead, as I mentioned I might. Did they arrive safely?

Yours affectionately,
              Lydia

Chapter III

Visitors: Expected and Otherwise

Joey was in a fever of excitement on Monday morning. Not only was her beloved sister due to arrive that evening, but she was also buoyed up by the prospect of driving to the station to meet Lydia and Rolf. She was almost too distracted to eat, imagining how much fun she and the Robin would have with Rolf—she supposed that he would be a younger version of her cousin George, who was her favourite among her aunts' families in London. She would have liked to go to the station to meet Madge, but Mr Maynard had vetoed this as Miss Bettany's train was not due to arrive until half-past eight that evening, so, reluctant to lose the chance of the drive, she had begged to meet the earlier train, and this had been allowed. The Robin, however, was to stay at home, as Miss Maynard was making her a new dress out of some pretty cotton that she had found in one of the attics, and it was ready to be fitted.

Punctually at three o'clock, the big car was waiting for Rolf and Lydia at Lyndhurst Road Station, and Joey had her nose pressed up against the window, eager to see the latest arrivals. A large trunk containing several beautiful dresses and smart suits had been sent on the week before, and the guests would just have travelling bags.

The train arrived on time, and the two travellers descended: a slim, fashionable woman, whose beauty was marred by an expression of discontent, and a sturdy, round, red-faced boy of about ten years old.

Even over the racket made by the engine as it prepared to leave the station, the boy's voice could be heard, petulantly expressing his feelings about the journey, and Joey pulled a face. Loud, high-pitched and thoroughly whiney, his tones made it clear that he did not in the least appreciate the treat of escaping the smoke and grime of Aldershot to spend his holidays in the countryside with his grandparents.

'Do come along, Rolf, please!' pleaded his mother. 'It will be tea-time soon, and you don't want to miss that, do you?' Lydia Maynard was well aware of her father-in-law's strictures regarding punctuality, and was determined that the week would at least start well in this regard.

'I don't want to come along!' retorted Rolf. 'I don't see why we should have to travel all the way here. I don't see why *they*,' and the contempt he injected into this word was considerable, 'shouldn't come and visit *us*. It's boring here—' Rolf had conveniently forgotten that he had been thoroughly bored at home as well—'and there's *nothing* to do.'

'Oh, darling,' sighed his mother, 'there's plenty to do. And two of Auntie Mollie's pupils are staying for Easter, with their headmistress. So you won't be bored at all, as you'll have someone of your own age to spend time with, and that will make a lovely change, won't it, dear? I'm sure Grandpapa will organise some expeditions to go on; perhaps to see the Rufus Stone? You enjoyed that, didn't you, last time?'

Indeed, young Rolf had thoroughly enjoyed the trip to the Rufus Stone on Boxing Day, although more due to its gory associations than anything else.

With his keen blue-grey eyes and thick crop of light-brown hair, Rolf bore more than a passing resemblance to his uncle, and was often mistaken for Jack Maynard's younger brother. The resemblance was, however, only on the surface. Years of being given his own way by an indulgent mother and a father who was absent all too often had turned young Rolf into a florid-skinned child with a petulant mouth. Rolf was the type of boy who missed being picked last for teams during games lessons only because he was an inveterate bully. A bully, but also a coward, who avoided tackling anyone at football if he possibly could, and disliked cricket as much because of the hard ball as anything else. He always claimed he had asthma, and couldn't run; and, indeed, his roundness made running a great effort and generally brought on enough breathlessness to prove his 'infirmity'.

'Please, Rolfie, be a good boy for Mother? I'll buy you a nice slab of chocolate if you do!' Lydia's expression had changed from discontent to pleading. She knew that her child was in line to inherit Pretty Maids one day, and also that Mr Maynard had an extremely dim view of his future heir; she rather suspected that he viewed Rolf's eventual inheritance of the estate with distaste. Any tardiness on their part due to Rolf's disobedience would not be smiled upon. At the same time, she was genuinely distressed to see her son looking unhappy. Lydia was possibly the only person in the world who believed that he really was a delicate child, and she would do everything in her power to avoid upsetting him, to the point of disobeying the orders of the doctor if she felt the medicine prescribed tasted so nasty as to do more actual harm than good. A mother's instinct, she felt, should not be denied.

Joey, sitting quietly in the car, raised her eyebrows, most unimpressed by this boorish individual who was open to *bribery*. Her schoolgirl sense of honour was deeply offended, and she was surprised, after the time she had spent with the Maynard family, that one of its members should be allowed to behave so badly in public.

At the suggestion of chocolate, Rolf's demeanour improved.

He knew that the planned sojourn at Pretty Maids was not really going to be boring; he had already heard that one of the pupils was a foreign child, much younger than he, and hence perfect for teasing, while he imagined that the older girl would be too much under the thumb of her sister, the Headmistress, to be much trouble (although he was a little in awe of the Headmistress herself, and thought of her with a capital letter). He therefore assumed his widest smile, and sauntered towards the car, airily greeting the driver with an admonishment to 'help my mother with the bags, my good man', before settling himself in the back. There he was somewhat taken aback to see Joey, who politely offered him her hand, and introduced herself.

'How do you do? I'm Joey Bettany.'

Rolf glanced back out of the car door, his aplomb somewhat diminished by this frank, straightforward and distinctly unexpected greeting. He glared at his mother, who was struggling with purse and luggage, and tottering on her high heels towards the station kiosk in order to purchase the promised bar of chocolate.

'Rolf Maynard,' he said gruffly, too surprised by her presence to say anything much for the time being.

Lydia Maynard duly appeared, handing the bar over with a hopeful, 'Now don't spoil your appetite by eating it all before we get there, dear,' which Rolf completely ignored. She politely greeted Jo, before checking her face in a small compact, powdering her pretty nose and resettling her fashionable pale green sisal hat on her blonde curls in preparation for their arrival.

Rolf amused himself during nursery supper by pulling faces at Joey and the Robin. While the Robin was slightly scared by the grimaces he produced, Miss Joey forgot her dignity so much as to retaliate, and, inspired by the gargoyles on Notre Dame which she had greatly admired on her visit to Paris the previous year, she contrived to outdo many of his efforts. She had already noticed his offhand treatment of the Robin that afternoon. Decidedly put out by Jo's arrival at the station in the Maynards' car, Rolf had shown off abominably much of the time, and had frequently pushed past both of them as they had walked round the grounds together, simply in order to prove that he was the most important guest at Pretty Maids. In holiday time, Rolf refused to do anything remotely resembling sport, such as playing clock golf or croquet: however, the Maynard family were insistent that he spend as much of his time outside as possible. Thus, the three children had trundled round the garden, with Rolf literally throwing his weight around, declaiming his opinions loudly and ignoring all overtures of friendship from the Robin. Joey couldn't bear anyone to be so cavalier in their treatment of her adopted sister, and, after the little girl had been sent to bed under the care of Miss Maynard, she gave Rolf the full force of her opinions.

'I think you have behaved in an extremely impolite and rude manner, considering that the Robin an' I are guests here,' she began, as they sat in the old day nursery.

'No, I haven't. I never do. You're the one who's rude, turning up in the car at the station, without so much as a by your leave. *I* shall inherit this house one day; therefore it is my pleasure—' with a distant memory of Henry VIII—'to behave the way I please,' returned Rolf, striding across the floor with his hands in his pockets, an attitude strictly forbidden both by his schoolmasters and his father, but indulged in at every opportunity. '*You're* being rude. You're being much ruder. You're being incredibly rude by daring to criticise my behaviour in my own home.' With each assertion, his voice rose slightly, in both pitch and volume.

'Ssssh! D'you want to bring everyone running in, to find out why you sound as though you're being murdered? You, you,'

Joey cast around for a suitable epithet, 'you Girl! You sound *exactly* like Simone, just before she starts boohooing!' She grinned maddeningly at him, the anticipation of an argument causing the blood to flow through her veins, and reddening her cheeks. Her eyes flashing, she advanced towards him.

What Joey didn't expect was Rolf's reaction to her taunt. Despite the fact that he neither knew nor cared who Simone was, he bellowed with hurt rage, and threw himself towards her. Although she was a head taller than he, by virtue of her extra years, Joey was slender to the point of thinness, and Rolf a good two stone the heavier. She staggered back under his weight, narrowly missing the sharp corner of the mantelpiece, and fetched up against the wall.

'What *do* you think you're doing?' she gasped.

She got no further, as the door opened to reveal Jack Maynard, who, knowing what a bully Rolf could be (he had caught the boy incinerating ants with the aid of a magnifying glass on more than one occasion), had decided to investigate the sound of raised voices. He stood surveying the scene, his blue-grey eyes cold and disdainful. Rolf and Joey both withered under his gaze, and Rolf dropped his hands and stepped backwards. He knew that his uncle would not thrash him, as one of his schoolmasters might, but that he had other ways to make life unpleasant during his stay.

'I am deeply ashamed of you, Rolf,' Jack Maynard began. 'That you should behave in such a manner not only to a girl, but also to a guest staying under our roof!'

Rolf looked defiant, but said nothing. Joey the straight felt that she ought to admit that she had played a large part in the argument, since she had provoked his behaviour. Under Jack's unrelenting gaze, however, she was loth to speak, and blushed deeply instead.

'Can you explain your behaviour? I shall be interested to hear what you have to say, although I find it hard to believe that anything you could tell me would excuse that kind of conduct.'

Rolf looked a little less defiant. His Uncle Jack and, to a lesser extent, his grandfather were the only two people within the family who consistently gave Rolf the discipline he needed. Captain Maynard was too often absent with his regiment, and Lydia too inclined to indulge the long-awaited child, aware that she was unable to have another, to give him the training he needed at home. At school, things were a little different; but frequent letters from his mother, continually taking his side in any petty dispute, undid most of the good that the school was trying to instil in him.

Both children now felt distinctly uncomfortable, Joey especially. Up until this moment, Jack Maynard had proven to be a delightful companion, being full of local lore and ideas for games. As children, he and his sister had explored the New Forest, visiting the gipsies and learning something of their language, as well as exercising the ancient rights of estover, or firewood collecting, that the Maynards had enjoyed for centuries. On one such expedition with Jo, he had told her how William I had requisitioned the land of the New Forest as a hunting preserve in 1079, and how the king had put out the eyes and removed the hands of those peasants who dared to disturb the animals. Joey and her host had cheerfully discussed this gruesome practice; and now, his ire thoroughly aroused, Jack Maynard seemed only too capable of imposing some similarly fearsome punishment on the two children standing before him.

Joey felt she could keep silent no longer. It was not pleasant to have to own up, but she was determined not to be a coward, whatever Rolf might be, and she knew she wasn't completely in the right. Rolf clearly was not going to answer his uncle's question and the silence was beginning to grow oppressive. Joey steeled herself to speak, and, plucking up her courage, opened her mouth.

'Mr Maynard—' she took a deep breath. 'It's partly my fault. I, um, I goaded him. I said—things.' She trailed off lamely, unsure of herself under Jack's gaze. 'I'm sorry,' she ventured, apologising to no-one in particular.

'Thank you, Joey. I am pleased to think that you have the decency and the courage to tell the truth.' He paused judicially, noticing the faint shadows under her eyes and her extreme pallor. 'You are worn out,' he continued, 'and I think that you should go to bed now. I shall ask Saunders to bring up some hot milk to help you sleep. You must put the light out directly you have finished it.'

Joey grimaced slightly, and Jack smiled inwardly at her reaction; the combination of an early night and hot milk was, he felt, ample justice, particularly since she had confessed her sins. She slipped out of the nursery and headed towards the pretty room she shared with the Robin; and, being careful not to wake the slumbering child, commenced her evening toilet.

'I am glad,' she thought, 'that I'm not there to see what's happening to Rolf. He may be a little horror, but Maynie's brother looked *exceedingly* fierce.' She was soon ready, and hopped into bed to await Saunders and the hot milk.

The next day saw a distinctly subdued Rolf at the breakfast table; and it is to be recorded that this was the one occasion in his life that he did *not* have to be rebuked for speaking with his mouth full. In fact, he did not utter one word during the meal, and dared not under the gimlet gaze of his uncle. He knew that any further misbehaviour would result in a sound thrashing and, more horrifyingly, that his father had given permission to Jack for such an undertaking, as it was beginning to dawn on Captain Maynard that his son was becoming entirely ungovernable under his current lax régime.

The silence round Rolf and his uncle, and, it must be added, Joey too, was barely noticeable. For the Robin, Madge's arrival while she was asleep eclipsed everything else, and she was overjoyed to be sharing breakfast with her Tante Marguérite, and pressed all kinds of delicacies on her until Madge was moved to protest.

'You should not pass the jam just to me, my angel! Let someone else have a chance to have some, too!'

'But I am *so* pleased to see you!' protested the Robin. 'Here is ze marmalade—' she used the French pronunciation—'instead. Do you wish more toast?'

Madge laughed. 'No, my dear child, I have quite enough as it is!'

At the opposite end of the table, Mr and Mrs Maynard were debating plans for the day with Mollie, while Lydia wondered in a mildly perturbed manner exactly *why* her son was being so quiet. She suspected it might be something to do with Jack, but decided not to pursue such a line of investigation since her brother-in-law looked so entirely forbidding, despite his comparative youth. Instead, she decided to enjoy the fact that Rolf was behaving himself without bribery, and joined in the discussion of the day's activities.

Pleasant though it might be to think that Rolf's silence was entirely due to Jack's influence, it must be confessed that much of it stemmed from a desire to gain revenge on Joey. He felt, not without some reason, that if she had not been present at Pretty Maids, his uncle's scathing lecture might well have been avoided. Unfairly, he blamed the entire episode on her, rather than his own ungoverned temper.

He was forced to reject most of his ideas as impractical; balancing buckets on doors and such like would only bring retribution during the inquest that was bound to follow such an upset, and he could not guarantee that Joey would be the one to be soaked. He required something rather more subtle than that. Helping himself to the last slice of toast, and ignoring the gentle suggestion from his grandmother that it would be more polite to offer it round the table first, he sank into a brown study.

It took him a day or so, since he was not used to thinking and found it something of an effort, but he finally hit on a plan. He had to wait a further day before he could put it into place, as he needed a ladder. Fortunately for him, he was able to bribe one of the gardener's boys to leave one of the short ladders outside 'accidentally' instead of putting it away safely for the night. In the meantime, he busied himself with locating the largest snail he could find in the grounds of Pretty Maids. All this preparation meant that the household experienced an unusual degree of peace, as he was very quiet in the interim.

At about three o'clock the next morning, the peace of the slumbering house was shattered by shrieks emanating from Joey and the Robin's room. Madge, who slept next door, was first on the scene, convinced that some ghastly accident had befallen one of her charges. Switching on the light, she saw the two girls sitting bolt upright in their beds, the Robin crying piteously.

'What is it—*qu'est-ce que c'est, ma petite*?' she asked, drawing the child close, and rocking her gently.

'*Un bruit vraiment affreux!*' hiccoughed the Robin. '*Écoute!*'

In the silence that followed, Joey, by now decidedly overwrought, crept over to the Robin's bed to join her sisters, while an eerie, high-pitched squeal penetrated the room from outside. It paused, and then sounded again. More they did not hear, as several other members of the household irrupted into the room, temporarily muffling the noises outside.

The sight of Lydia in shingle cap and cold cream did more to restore Joey to her normal senses than any amount of petting might have done, and she was soon able to describe what had happened, in answer to their questioning. The Robin's sobs had by now subsided to very gentle hiccoughs, as she was wrapped in her blankets and safely rocked in Madge's arms.

'I was fast asleep, when I woke up to hear the most *gruesome* squealing sounds just outside the window. I lay there, too scared to move 'cos they were so utterly ghastly, and then the Robin let out that terrible yowl, and you all came in!' Joey shuddered visibly, and Miss Maynard came to comfort her.

Rolf was gently hugging himself, and biting his lip to keep from laughing. He was, as might easily be guessed, at the root of this trouble, and he had not even in his wildest dreams imagined that it might result in such a wholesale rousing of the household.

Jack Maynard, meanwhile, walked purposefully to the window, and flung open the curtains, intending to prove to the frightened children that there was no danger. Silhouetted against the moonlight, clearly visible to all present, an enormous snail was creeping across the window-pane. As it humped its body, a high pitched whine, magnified by the glass, was clearly audible; and, as it flattened its body to move further forward, the pitch and volume changed to a tone that was, particularly if it wakened one in the night, truly ghastly. Rolf had found a smaller snail performing a similar feat on the glasshouse, and it was this that had inspired him to pay Joey back in such a truly original manner. That the Robin would be affected too made no difference to him. He was entirely unmoved by the angelic beauty of that small person, and had rejected all the overtures of friendship she had made to him that week, much to her surprise, as she regarded the whole world as her friend.

Greatly relieved by the discovery that it was, after all, only a snail, both Joey and the Robin were persuaded to go back to sleep. Meanwhile, Jack Maynard leant out of the window in a most athletic manner to knock the unwanted visitor from its promenade. To be on the safe side, hot milk was brewed by no less a person than Mrs Maynard, and the girls were both excused the morning service at church the next day, and attended Evensong with Madge instead—although the Robin was Catholic like her mother, she had been given permission by her father, Captain Humphries, to attend church with the Bettanys.

The day's plans were still carried out, first searching for the brightly dyed eggs which Mr Maynard had hidden cunningly all round the house and garden, and then rolling them down a short slope to see whose egg would reach the bottom first, guaranteeing its owner happiness throughout the year. Rolf enjoyed the hunt as much as the rest of them—he had very little conscience and did not feel at all guilty for causing the disturbances during the night. He was put out to discover that Joey had found more eggs than he had, and even more so when she shared most of them with the Robin and her sister, giving only one to him. However, this egg rolled down the hill faster than any of the others, and he was slightly mollified.

Chapter IV

THE FIRST DAY OF TERM

'JOEY, Jo-ey!' A fair girl, with flaxen plaits flying, came running across the cricket pitch towards the big Chalet, where Joey was standing in the great doorway next to her sister, greeting her fellow-pupils as they returned to the school. The journey back to the Tyrol had passed without incident, and the Bettanys had settled quickly back into school ready for the new term.

Joey turned and waved, before looking up at her sister and, on receiving a nod of agreement, sped across the field towards her friend, closely followed by her St Bernard, Rufus.

'Frieda, how simply topping to see you again! Why haven't you been over to see us earlier?'

'We were in Innsbruck until yesterday. Die Grossmutter was not well, so we were unable to come earlier,' replied the pretty Tyrolean, kneeling to make a fuss of the dog.

'Oh, I'm sorry,' said Joey. She greatly respected the old lady, who was extremely frail and well into her nineties. 'How is she now?'

'Very much better. She was not very ill, but der Vater felt that we should not all move up to Seespitz until she was quite, quite well again.' Frieda sighed, then changed the subject to matters school related. 'How many new girls have we this term?'

'Not as many as last, although there are plenty to come. Ma— My sister'—Joey invariably spent most of the first week of term with a slight stammer as she remembered just too late that she was not supposed to refer to her sister by her first name during term time—'wants them to start in the autumn term rather than the summer. It's more usual in English schools, y'know. But we've got a new Senior now, whom we know from Devon—that's Mary Burnett. She's Rosalie Dene's cousin, but didn't come at the same time as Rosalie because she had scarlet fever. Then there are two more for us: one of 'em, Cyrilla Maurús, is Hungarian, so heaven only knows how we'll talk to her, although I'm sure we'll manage in time like we did with Ingeborg and Thyra Eriksen in Le Petit Chalet; and then the tinies have a French kid called Honorine, who was at the same school as Simone and Renée. Mary was a Guide in Taverton where we used to live, and I think she's got her Second Class and is working all out for her First Class, and we must find out what the other girls have done in the way of Guiding.' Joey was forced to pause for breath at this point in her somewhat long-winded explanation, as she had been talking non-stop as they walked across the grass.

'And how is Madame?' inquired Frieda.

'Very well indeed. She had a ripping time at Foxlease, the Guiding place, and we're to start meetings on Saturday morning!'

'Oh, *good*!' replied Frieda. She and her sister had turned their attention from the English school stories with which they were plentifully supplied by their father to Guiding stories (along with one or two books about the Camp Fire movement, since Herr Mensch was slightly bewildered by the various English youth movements), and had spent their time over the holidays learning how the Union Jack is made up, and practising various knots and the Morse Code, all in preparation for the new term's adventure.

By this time they had reached the entrance to the school, and both curtseyed to Madame as they passed through the door, Frieda answering her headmistress's inquiries as to her health and that of her sister, Bernhilda, and the rest of her family.

Immediately inside the hall they were met by their

contemporaries Simone Lecoutier and Marie von Eschenau, and together the quartette went through to the big Saal where the school was assembled—there was no need for Frieda to unpack since, during the summer, she and Bernhilda, along with several other girls who had families living round the lakeside, were day pupils. In the Saal, Mademoiselle bade them sit and wait for Madame, who was greeting the final few arrivals and sending them to their dormitories to leave their cases before congregating in the bright, airy room. The new matron would supervise their unpacking after the school had assembled.

The Middles quickly seated themselves on the wooden chairs set out in the middle of the hall. The prefects were arranged to the right hand of the Head in wicker chairs, with the Staff on her left, while the rest of the Seniors sat at the back, also on wicker chairs, and the Juniors curled up on the floor at the front. A gentle, polyglot babble rose from the girls as they debated exactly *what* the new mistress seated on the platform might teach, and, as the last of their number joined them, silence fell as Miss Bettany followed after her and walked towards the small raised platform at the end of the room.

'Good afternoon, girls,' she began in her low, musical voice. 'Welcome back to the Chalet School. I never thought, when I began the school a year ago, that there would be quite so many of you this term! I am particularly pleased to welcome our new pupils: I hope you will be very happy with us!

'As you can see, we also have two new members of staff. This is Miss Carthew,' here she indicated a tall, graceful-looking woman, with dark hair and deep hazel eyes, 'who will teach history throughout the school, and will be living in Le Petit Chalet. We also have, for the first time, a matron, Miss Wilson, who comes to us from a large boys' school in Durham; please try not to shock her too much, as she is not used to so many girls yet! If ever any of you feel ill, you are to go to Matron first, and she will look after you. We have made a small san at the top of the Chalet, where she will sleep, and you may go to her at any hour of the day or night if there is an emergency. Woe betide you, however, should you disturb her sleep for something that isn't an emergency!' and Miss Bettany smiled at her pupils. They were very impressed by the crisp looking lady sitting on the dais, her hair almost entirely hidden beneath her 'angels' wings' cap. She looked very strict, and likely, as Jo said later, 'to dose you with the vilest tonic ever'.

'Next term we are planning to divide you up into forms, and your work this term will go a good way to affecting which form you are in. It will not simply be a matter of where you are positioned in the end-of-term exams: we want you to work steadily throughout the term.' At these words, two of the Middles, Evadne Lannis and Margia Stevens, grinned inwardly. Bosom pals, they had distinctly different working styles. Evadne, child of an indulgent American who had married a local Austrian girl, was prone to working in fits and starts, while Margia, daughter of a journalist from one of the London papers, tended to work diligently. She hoped to be a concert pianist in the future, and her piano master, Herr Anserl, insisted that she work conscientiously at her playing. This had affected her approach to her other lessons also. That Evadne was a year older than Margia would probably be cancelled out by her poor performance in class, and it sounded as though they could look forward to remaining together for a while longer.

'I have one final announcement. We shall be starting Guides this term. Most of you know what I mean by this; for the new girls who perhaps have not had the chance to join the Sisterhood of Guiding in their own countries, I shall explain a little more.

'Guiding is quite a new movement, which started after a group of girls decided that they wished to have the fun of Scouting that their brothers enjoyed. It is an organisation for character training, aiming to help girls learn how to be women—self-helpful, happy, prosperous, prepared for all eventualities and capable of keeping good homes and bringing up good children. I have written to all your parents, and explained all about it, and all have agreed to allow you to join.'

The girls could not quite contain their excitement at this announcement, and they nudged each other with delighted grins, unable to sit still. Before their quiet murmurs could become an excited babble, the Head Girl, Gisela, rose to express their feelings in an eminently suitable manner.

'Three cheers for Miss Bettany and Guiding!' she cried, as she sprang to her feet, and forgetting her usual shyness, such was her enthusiasm for the Guides. 'Hip! Hip!'

'Hurrah!' cried the School, cheering with all its might, and creating more noise than might reasonably be expected from a group of only about forty girls. Miss Bettany let them have their way for a moment, then laughingly quelled the commotion by holding up her hand for silence, which fell instantly.

'Of course,' she continued, smiling down at the Juniors who were clustered near her feet, 'not all of you are old enough to be Guides. However, Miss Durrant was a Brown Owl in England, and I am pleased to announce that she and Miss Carthew will lead a Brownie Pack for you younger folk while the older girls are enjoying Guides.'

The clouds that had been crossing the faces of some of the small fry at the beginning of this announcement were immediately dispelled as they broke into large beaming smiles, those who were unsure as to the exact nature of Brownies taking their cue from those who were better informed.

'Your first meetings will be on Saturday morning, and we

55

shall explain more then. For the first week, we shall give over the whole day to Guides, so that you can have as great a taste as possible of what Guiding is. I am sure that many of you have been practising for your Tenderfoot test over the holidays.' At this, one or two girls looked slightly dismayed, since they still had only the vaguest idea of what was required of them. 'Those of you who were Brownies or Guides at home, please wear your uniforms for the initial meeting. Everyone else's uniforms will arrive soon, I hope!

'I shall not keep you any longer; I am sure that the prefects wish to meet and discuss duties before *Abendessen*. Le Petit Chalet will go straight to *Abendessen* now; the rest of the school will have it in half an hour. After that, we will have Prayers and then the Middles will go straight to bed. Seniors may stay up half an hour longer. Many of you have had a long and tiring journey to come here over the past two days, and you will be grateful for a long sleep. Mademoiselle!'

Mademoiselle La Pâttre, a homely Frenchwoman whose features contrasted greatly with her Headmistress's delicate prettiness, struck up a jolly march on the piano, and the girls marched smartly out of the room. The prefects headed straight to their meeting, and the Juniors were taken over to their own house, Le Petit Chalet, under the care of Miss Durrant. The Middles and Seniors divided into their own rooms, and immediately began discussing Miss Bettany's announcement about the Guides.

From the moment that Grizel Cochrane had returned from England the previous term, armed with copies of two of the Guide handbooks, *Girl Guiding* and *Girl Guide Badges and How to Win Them*, and several story books on the same subject, the pupils of the Chalet School had been keen to start their own Guide company. Grizel had generously lent her books all round the Seniors and Middles: always attracted by anything new,

THE FIRST DAY OF TERM

she had learnt all she could about the Guides and was especially keen that the others should join her in her new preoccupation. Of particular interest to the girls had been the Arts and Crafts badges, while the cooking and housewifery knowledge required for the tests seemed matter of course, as many of the girls' mothers did the housekeeping themselves. Most of them were less keen on the nursing tests, but knots appealed, as they saw the value of learning them, living as they did in a mountainous district where ropes were in constant use. They also saw the point of signalling and being able to estimate heights and distances accurately.

In the Senior common room Grizel was busy pumping her old friend Mary Burnett for information: Grizel, Joey, Rosalie and Mary had all attended the same school in Taverton, and encouraged by Mr Dene—a keen Scout himself—both Mary and Rosalie had joined a Guide company in the town. Mary had been a Guide for some time, and already had experience of two companies, for she had transferred from the 1st Taverton to the High School's 3rd Taverton when it started. Rosalie, on the other hand, had spent less than a year as a Guide before she had joined the Chalet School. Even this, however, had been enough to give her a certain cachet among the Chalet girls: apart from the staff, they were the only members of the School who had earned the right to wear the brass trefoil badge of the Guides.

'The most difficult thing,' Mary stated firmly, 'is Morse. It's absolutely impossible, and I had the dickens of a job learning it.' She grimaced at the memory, screwing up her pleasant face and frowning portentously.

'Mary, you shouldn't use language like that! I'm sure that "dickens of a job" is slang, and Madame is very keen that we don't use such language!' Rosalie looked faintly shocked. 'I did warn you during the holidays. Madame says that in a school made up of so many different nationalities, it is important that we use correct English.'

'Sorry. I just keep forgetting.'

'You just keep forgetting, and you'll soon just have no money, as we get fined for using slang!'

'I'll try. Anyhow, Morse is horribly hard, and it kept lots of us in 3rd Taverton from gaining our Second Class badges—including me for a while,' Mary continued ruefully. 'It was the one clause that kept me from getting my Second Class during my first term.'

'And then you can start on the badges, can't you? Once you've got your Second Class, I mean,' Grizel put in. 'Which did you do first?'

'Oh, I earned Cook first, but we also worked on Ambulance and Needlewoman. They're all ones that you need for First Class, you know. Although,' she added thoughtfully, 'I should like to do the Interpreter badge too, now that I'm here. I sometimes think that I'd like to be a languages mistress, when I'm older.'

'Very practical,' returned Grizel. 'I can see the point of getting the First Class badges out of the way first. What about you, Stéphanie? Were you a Guide in France?'

Stéphanie Pagnol looked up, startled, her periwinkle-blue eyes wide open.

'In France? *Mais non!* You forget, Grizel, that I was at school in Vienna, before Maman became ill. Besides, Maman and *ma tante* did not think it was proper for us to join *les Éclaireuses* in France. They work very much with poor people, so we did not join. However, this term, I shall be a Guide, and attend the meetings on Saturday morning before Aurélie and I go up to the Sonnalpe to visit Maman.' Madame Pagnol had moved up to a chalet on the Sonnalpe during the Easter holidays, the Sanatorium not yet being open, as Dr Russell felt that her health would benefit from the cleaner air and higher altitude.

'What say you, Rosalie? You were a Guide with Mary. What else have you got to do for Second Class?'

'Most of it, I'm afraid. I only had one term at Guides, and that was the summer term—after that I came here—so we spent most of our time tackling the outdoorsy things. So, I've done the observation, and I can stalk and track, and light a fire and run a mile, but I've still to learn Morse and do all the ambulance work.' She sighed. 'Mary's right. Morse is definitely the worst part of it.'

'Oh, it's not so bad,' replied Grizel, who had been practising solidly during the Easter holiday.

'That's easy for you to say, my dear. You're musical! All those rhythmic exercises give you a natural advantage!'

As soon as the Middles reached their room, they too began to question the newcomers as to their experience with Guides, just in case someone else knew more than they did. Aurélie Pagnol found herself bombarded with questions and information, as she had missed many of the previous term's discussions since her cousin Stéphanie had been much wanted at home because of her mother's illness, and Aurélie had perforce remained with her. Cyrilla Maurús, the Hungarian girl, was entirely mystified, not having encountered the Girl Scouts, as they are called in Hungary, but Aurélie, after some initial confusion, grasped what excited the Middles so much.

'The Guy-des?' she queried, brows knotted as she essayed the correct pronunciation.

'Oh, in French it's *les Éclaireuses*!' clarified Joey.

'I think,' began Aurélie, 'that my friend in Marseilles has worked with the poor girls there, for *les Éclaireuses*, but it is not something that *ma tante* thought proper *pour Stéphanie et moi*, since it is a movement non-religious and we are Catholics.' Aurélie used the French pronunciation for these words, her accent not yet ironed out by her time at the School. 'I believe, in Paris, there are *les Guides de France*, but not in Le Midi. Then, of course, we moved to *Wien*, and there are not the Guy-des there,' and, with a little shrug, she ended her speech.

'Oh, but you must join us!'

'Ma— My sister says that everyone can join!'

'It is for *everyone*.'

'An' we will have heaps of fun, and do such jolly, topping things, and go camping, and cook on open fires, and track, and learn how to keep bees, and milk cows, and hike. It will be glorious!' This was Jo, her imagination beginning to run away with her a little.

'Oh, where do you think we're going to keep a cow? With Rufus? Don't be such an ass!' retorted Evadne.

Jo bristled in return, but decided that this was not worth bickering over.

Aurélie looked a little doubtful. It all sounded very outdoors to her, and, since her aunt was staying up at the Sonnalpe for her health, she was not sure that her own health would allow her to participate. *Messieurs les docteurs* would certainly have something to say to her cousin, as they feared she might inherit her mother's ill health.

'It is, per'aps, not very *comme il faut*?'

'It's as *comme il faut* as can be!' retorted Joey, hotly. 'You can't get much more proper than a Guide!'

'And it is not all outdoors, either,' interjected Frieda, who guessed that Aurélie was feeling overwhelmed by the open-air aspect of the movement. 'We will also learn to sew practical garments, and to cook, and look after children, and launder, and how to care for our homes in the future.'

Aurélie smiled. This sounded rather more to her taste, and she agreed to try. Cyrilla, however, was completely confused by all the explanations, until Joey, poring over the copies of *Girl Guiding* and *Girl Guide Badges* that Miss Bettany had brought back from England, tried to explain what it was that they needed to do.

"'Tenderfoot Test. Must know—'" Joey read, and took a deep breath—"'the Guide Law, the threefold promise, the signs and salute, must understand the composition of the Union Jack and the right way to fly it.'"

'Right way?' inquired Simone, her dark head bent next to Joey's.

'Shh! "Must be able to tie four of the following knots and know their uses:– Reef, sheet-bend, clove-hitch, bowline, fisherman's and sheepshank; must have one month's attendance."'

'Right way for the flag?'

'Right way: so that it's not upside down. If it's upside down, it's a signal that you're in distress and need rescuing,' Joey explained. 'You see, the Union Jack's made up of the three flags of St George, St Andrew and St Patrick, and St Andrew has the more honourable position nearest the flag pole while St Patrick has the same on the other side.' Joey's explanation, though factually correct, left Simone none the wiser, and she stared blankly. 'See!' and Joey pointed out the page in the book. The continental girls crowded over to see, and jostled her elbow.

'Hey there! Gently does it! Take care of it!' Joey the book lover had been brought up to respect books and look after them.

'Oh, I see!' Frieda nodded sagely. 'So the flag is made up of the three different flags of England, Ireland and Scotland.' She thought for a moment. 'What about Wales?'

'I don't think Wales has a flag. I think it might have a standard with a red dragon on it—at least, I remember seeing a picture of the Prince of Wales' investiture, and there were lots of standards with dragons on in that.'

'Perhaps the dragon is in the middle of the red cross of St George,' suggested Margia, who had a poetical mind. 'It's there, but you can't see it.'

'We shall have to ask Bill, during geography, or perhaps Miss Carthew. It might be a historical reason. Anyhow. Then, before we can do any Guide badges, we have to get Second Class. Shall I read that as well?'

'Oh, no, Joey. There's quite enough to think about for Tenderfoot tests! Besides, if we're to have four weeks' attendance before we can make our promises, that takes us nearly half-way through the term,' replied Margia.

'I guess there'll be plenty of time to think about Second Class after that,' added Evadne, tilting back on her chair.

'Do you think so? What about Morse?' Joey tapped a pencil, seemingly idly as she spoke.

'Plenty of time for that too!'

'Then you didn't realise that I tapped out "Morse" in Morse just then?'

Evadne's chair crashed upright with a thud.

'Really?'

'Yes, really! I've been practising whenever I could during the holidays. Maynie helped, of course, as she's a Lieutenant in the Guides. 'S hard, even so, and I still get muddled.'

Evadne groaned, and shook her head. 'I shall never get it.'

Later, in the staffroom, as the staff relaxed with coffee and a selection of delicious biscuits which Mademoiselle had brought back from Paris, they discussed the term ahead. Mademoiselle, looking to the future, wondered how long it would be before her Headmistress married and moved to the Sonnalpe.

'Oh, Mademoiselle, I shall be Headmistress for at least year yet: Dr Russell and I won't be married until the Sanatorium is well and truly established, and the building work hasn't even been started. He and Captain Humphries—when he's there—are almost camping in their chalet at present. When we do marry, I shall retire—the Sonnalpe's simply too far away for me to come down and teach on a regular basis, particularly in the winter.'

'Och, but the first patients are beginning to arrive up at the Sonnalpe, are they not?' prompted Matron.

'Just a handful, yes. Mr Denny has, I gather, already moved up there, as the doctors believe it will improve his health; and Stéphanie's mother and one or two others have gone as well. However, they are exceptions—it really is necessary for them to be there.'

Miss Bettany sipped her coffee, and reached for another biscuit. Although sylph-like in figure, she was able to match her younger sister's appetite—Joey had been known to out-eat the rest of the School's pupils on picnics—and these delicacies were particularly mouth-watering.

'Joey, Juliet and the Robin all know that they are not to mention my engagement to the other girls until I say so. I don't want to announce anything until I'm absolutely sure when the wedding will be; otherwise the entire school will be on tenterhooks for far too long, and that's sure to breed unrest!'

'I quite agree, Madame,' replied Miss Maynard. 'I think they'll have more than enough to amuse themselves with Guides, without adding any more excitements! Another biscuit, Miss Wilson?' she asked, turning to the new Matron.

'Thank you. Perhaps just one more before I turn in!' she smiled back. 'I feel absolutely exhausted—it must be the air! Or perhaps it's all the chattering. Girls are definitely much more high-pitched than boys!' She laughed, her starched angels' wings cap bobbing.

Mademoiselle rose to leave. 'I must return to Le Petit Chalet. I cannot leave Miss Durrant alone over there for much longer. Although I do not imagine that there might be any type of disaster, particularly on the first night, I think I would rather be there than here. *Bonne nuit, mes amies!*'

'I should turn in too,' replied Miss Maynard. 'I think I'm going to sleep like a log tonight! Goodnight everyone! Sweet dreams!'

The rest of the staff finished their coffee, and Matron departed kitchenwards with the tray of empty cups. Before long, the whole Chalet was slumbering peacefully, from the Headmistress in her little room to Rufus, Joey's beloved St Bernard, in the outhouse.

Chapter V

GUIDES!

THE school as a whole was bubbling with excitement on Saturday morning, and it should be recorded that never again were the girls ready for *Frühstück* so quickly. They raced through their baths, emerging glowing from the icy sting of the mountain water, stripped their beds at record speed, and hung their plumeaux over the balconies of the dormitories so that the soft, eiderdown-like bedcovers could air. It was a beautiful May day, and, after some consultation over the breakfast table, Miss Bettany and Miss Maynard, in their capacities as the Captain and the Lieutenant of the company respectively, decided that the afternoon would be given over to tracking games, and in the evening they would make the patrol flags.

Three times during the course of this discussion it was necessary for the Headmistress to ring the small silver bell which indicated to the girls that their chatter was becoming too noisy for comfort. On the third occasion, she felt moved to speak.

'Girls! Please be a little quieter! I am sure that you can be heard up on the Sonnalpe! I know that you are excited, but if you continue to talk at such a volume, I shall have to postpone your Guide meeting for at least a week, until you have calmed down a little!'

There was a general frisson of horror amongst the girls: the idea of losing their meeting was too terrible to contemplate. Joey opened her mouth to protest, and then shut it rapidly, knowing that her sister might well carry through her threat were she so to do. Miss Bettany, however, had no serious intention of postponing the meeting. She knew her pupils well enough to gauge that such a threat would ensure, if not silence, at least peace.

'Thank you!' she smiled, when the girls had settled down again. 'Please all finish your *Kaffee*, and, when you have done so, go and make your beds. As you know, we shall meet in Hall at nine-thirty prompt! I expect you all to be as smart as possible, and to wait *quietly*. Remember that "A Guide's Honour is to be Trusted", and I trust you to carry out my instructions.'

Within twenty minutes, all the girls, including the day pupils, were waiting in the big hall. They were arranged in an approximate horseshoe, as directed by Grizel, with the aid of Rosalie and Mary, who were both well used to performing this ceremony in the Taverton Guides.

Grizel was determined to make a success of the new Guide company. Whilst living in Taverton, she had remained in almost complete ignorance of the movement, largely because the nearest company had been located at some distance from her home. Though it had been quite possible for her to attend Taverton High School during the day, it had proved too difficult for her to travel alone to a different part of the town at night and her stepmother had been unable to provide her with transport. Since then, however, the High School had formed its own company, much to the delight of the girls in Grizel's old form. They had not been slow to communicate their enthusiasm to Grizel, and as a result she was as keen on the subject now as once she had been indifferent. The prospect of Guides was attractive in the extreme, and Miss Bettany hoped that it would help to round out a character that was inclined to be selfish and wilful.

As she stood in the horseshoe waiting for her Captain and her Lieutenant, Grizel's vivid face was becomingly flushed, and she rivalled even Wanda von Eschenau for beauty at that moment.

Her normal tendency to fight for her own hand first had metamorphosed into a desire to do her best as a Guide, and for her company. She stood erect and proud, determined to prove herself.

Punctually at nine-thirty Miss Bettany, in her uniform as Guide Captain, accompanied by Miss Maynard as Lieutenant, entered the room. The green warrant badge brooch just below the knot of her light blue tie, along with the navy blue cockade on the left side of her hat, proclaimed her rank, while her Tenderfoot brooch was on her left breast. Miss Maynard wore the same uniform, but without the cockade and with her Tenderfoot brooch on the left of her hat, with a gilt warrant badge brooch just below the knot of her tie.

Miss Bettany smiled at the ragged horseshoe shape, recognising it for what it was, and saluted her company.

'Good morning, Guides. Welcome to the first meeting of the 1st Tiern See Guide Company. We have a great deal to do this morning as, apart from explaining the Guide movement to you, I also want to divide you into patrols, begin your Tenderfoot work and explain the secret signs of the Guides. This afternoon we shall play some scouting games—that is to say, games that teach searching and "scouting" about—and after *Kaffee und Kuchen*, you will make your patrol flags. Guiding is more than a terrific game; it goes far deeper. The skills you will learn as Guides will remain with you for the rest of your lives.'

As the girls listened intently, she explained the history of the Guide Movement, the Promise and the Laws, the patrol system, the badges each girl could train for and earn, and what it meant to be a Guide. Then she announced the patrols.

'We shall have four patrols. The leader of the first will be Juliet Carrick and that of the second, Rosalie Dene. The third will be led by Gertrud Steinbrücke and the last by Grizel

Cochrane. Their seconds are, respectively, Bette Rincini, Vanna di Ricci, Mary Burnett and Luigia di Ferrara. Gisela, Bernhilda and Wanda will form a patrol of Senior Guides—they have a great deal of responsibility already, and are very busy with their duties as prefects. I have lists of the remaining members of the patrols, and the first thing you will need to do as a patrol is to decide what to call yourselves. Choose wisely: you will want to decorate your log book with your emblem, as well as wearing it as your patrol badge and its colours in your shoulder knot.'

Earlier in the week, Miss Bettany had discussed the idea of a senior patrol with the three eldest girls in the school. She knew that they were as keen as everyone else to join the Guides, but had to temper their keenness with the fact that they were only to be at the school for one more term. Furthermore, although her three head prefects were the eldest of the girls, and had a great deal of influence over their fellow-pupils, they had no more knowledge of Guiding than the Robin.

Considering what she had said, Gisela spoke for them all.

'I think, Madame, that it is perhaps more important that we devote our energies to leading the school, rather than leading the Guides?'

'Yes, that's exactly it. I think you might be happier just being Guides, without the extra responsibility that comes with being a Patrol Leader.'

'And, of course, we know very little about Guiding, while Rosalie is already a Guide, and would make a much better Patrol Leader,' added Bernhilda, who really knew more than she thought she did, having read so many stories during the holidays.

'That is true as well. I want you to be able to enjoy your last term at school, and so I would like you to become a senior patrol, separate from the others, but taking part fully in all the activities.

Would you like to do that? You would be similar to what we call "Rangers" in England—older Guides who "Look Wider" and are more aware of the world around them.'

And they had agreed, forming the Honesty patrol.

The rest of the Guides were quickly allocated to the four patrols, with Margia and Evadne finding themselves separated. The two French cousins, Stéphanie and Aurélie, who had been standing very close to each other, were also separated: Stéphanie was to be in Grizel's patrol, and Aurélie was with Joey, under Juliet's leadership. Joey was far less likely to argue with Juliet, whom she regarded as akin to a sister, than she was with Grizel. Grizel, therefore, found that Simone was to be an ornament of her patrol, along with Frieda. The Captain and Lieutenant felt that Joey would enjoy Guides far more if Simone were not hanging on her every word, as was her custom if at all possible. The Guiders had not made these decisions lightly, but rejoiced that Guides gave them the opportunity to allow each individual pupil to blossom in a way that was not always easily achieved during school hours.

Settled in their patrol corners, the fledgling Guides debated the various patrol names, running through the lists in the handbook, and then voting on their favourites, usually according to whether they liked the sound of the shoulder knots that they would wear on their uniforms.

'Cock, oh, please, cock for us!' cried Margia. 'Brown and red shoulder knot is so similar to our School colours! Do write it down, Gertrud, please!'

And so Gertrud did.

On the other side of the room, Jo was equally vociferous in her request for the Scarlet Pimpernel to be considered, as she was inspired by that elusive Pimpernel of literature, and the scarlet shoulder knot was beguiling. However, she was outvoted by the rest of the group, and they became the Poppies, with a dark green and red shoulder knot.

No one seemed sure whether they had to choose between all flower names and all birds, but when the patrols eventually reconvened, there were found to be two birds—the Swallows, who would sport a dark-blue-and-white shoulder knot under the leadership of Rosalie, and the Cocks under the leadership of Gertrud—while Grizel led the Cornflowers with their neat royal blue shoulder knot, and Juliet was charged with the care of the Poppies.

Next, they discussed their Tenderfoot challenges. While all the English girls had a fair knowledge of how the Union Jack was made up, the continental girls found this hard; and the English girls in turn knew very little about the continental girls' flags—as British Guides in a foreign country they would have to know about all the flags represented in the company in order to pass their Tenderfoot tests. The girls found this a daunting idea, as there were as many as seven different nations represented in the company.

This was followed by a game of 'Guide's Nose', during which each Guide was given three bags in turn, each containing a different smelling article such as coffee, rose petals or aniseed, and asked to identify them. This provoked much mirth, as Joey, infected with a sense of the dramatic, sniffed loudly at each bag she was given, before announcing, in the manner of Alice in Wonderland's Duchess, that it contained 'Pepper!' In fact, they contained custard powder, crushed parma violets and cloves, and Miss Bettany threatened to send her younger sister to Matron to have her sinuses washed out.

A lively game of 'Port and Starboard' followed, giving the girls a chance to run off some of the surplus energy resulting from sitting for so long. Finally, they reassembled in a more professional-looking horseshoe, each patrol with its Leader at one end and its Second at the other, with the rest of its members lined up between, just as they should be.

Miss Bettany held up her right hand for complete silence.

'Remember, Guides, that the promise you will all make in a few weeks' time is extremely important. It is not a selection of words to be mumbled unthinkingly; when you make your promise, you must mean every word you say. After all, being a Guide is not about dressing up in smart plumage, and sewing decorations on to your clothes. You promise to do your *best* to do your duty to God and the King or your country, your *best* to help other people at *all* times, and your *best* to obey every one of the Guide Laws. If you try your hardest, you will succeed in this; although you would be superhuman if you succeeded every time! We want you to be proud of your company, and justly so.'

The girls stood silent for a moment, before Gisela took the initiative: as Head Girl she well recognised her duty as spokeswoman for the rest of the School.

'I am sure I speak for us all when I say that we shall try, Captain.'

'Thank you. Company dismissed! Be ready on the playing field in your gym slips at fourteen-thirty.'

Half-past two, or fourteen-thirty, saw the Senior school ready on the cricket pitch, arrayed in their gym tunics and raring to go. Ideas abounded as to what the Captain and Lieutenant had in mind, but the girls were generally agreed that it was to be some sort of tracking game. They did not have to wait long to find out.

'Guides, we are going to start off with a game of "Judging Time", to see how good you are at estimating the passing of time,' began Miss Bettany. 'You will go off in pairs for a specified interval, and return to us when you think your time is up; and we'll mark you according to your success. You are on your honour not to consult any watches. If you think you may be tempted, you may leave your watch with the Lieutenant.' Miss Bettany felt rather self-conscious referring to her colleague in this way, and even more self-conscious at being addressed as 'Captain', despite the fact that it was a well-earned title.

'After this, we will have a "Quick Sight Race", where we'll send you out in different directions to observe all you can in the way of tracks, trees, flowers, landmarks and so on in fifteen minutes. The pair with the most correct observations will win a small prize!'

The girls smiled at each other, many of them still being at the 'pot-hunting' stage, and keen to win any type of glory at all. Laughing and chattering, they dispersed in the different directions pointed out to them by the Captain and Lieutenant. Most of the girls were able to estimate their time away to within three minutes, which was very good for a beginning. Frieda and Simone, however, distinguished themselves by returning within thirty seconds of their allotted seven minutes; they had achieved this by counting to themselves very quietly, seven times, up to sixty; a clever ruse which some of the other Middles determined to try when next they played the game (and which the Lieutenant vowed to scotch by suggesting time periods of up to twenty minutes on the next occasion).

Then came the observation game. In order to make sure that the girls spent as much of the fifteen minutes as possible observing, rather than counting, there was to be a whistle blown when there were five minutes, three minutes and one minute left before returning to 'home'. The Seniors were allowed to move outside the school grounds, being trusted by their Captain and Lieutenant to return promptly within the time allowed, while the Middles were bounded by the big withe fence.

They all ran off at the highest speed, determined to cover as much ground as possible. There was peace for ten minutes or so, and then the first whistle was blown. By the time there was only one minute left, only Joey, Margia and Evadne, who had been sent off as a group of three, remained away from the Chalet. Surrounded by a group of excited Guides when the time was up, Miss Maynard and Miss Bettany did not at first notice this, as they were so busy listening to each group, and marking their observations against lists that they themselves had made during the week.

Realising that they were late, the three were heading back to the Chalet with all possible speed. Suddenly, Margia overbalanced, letting out a frightful shriek, as she hit a tussock of unusually long, lush grass and tumbled over. She landed with a distinct thump and immediately paled. Evadne, pulling up suddenly behind her, narrowly missed tripping over her friend, and teetered on the tips of her toes before managing to right herself.

'Say, are you OK?' she asked anxiously. 'You came a right cropper just now!'

Margia bravely tried to hold back the tears prickling dangerously at the corners of her eyes. She began to nod but this quickly turned into a shake as, getting up from the ground, she jarred her left foot painfully.

'N-no,' she gasped. 'I've hurt my ankle. Gosh, it hurts!' With this she sank back down to the ground.

Evadne surveyed her with a sympathetic air.

'Guess we'd better get you back to the Chalet, so's Matron can have a look at it. Can you stand if I help you?'

Margia shook her head, biting her lip.

'No, it really is painful! Even thinking about moving it hurts!'

Margia desperately wanted to cry, but a Guide, as she had learned, 'smiles and sings under all difficulties'. She racked her brain to try and think of a song, but was only able to come up with 'London Bridge is falling down', which mirrored her own situation rather too closely. Fortunately, Joey caught up with them at that point, and provided an alternative distraction.

'What's up?' she asked, seeing the rest of her team brought to an unexpected halt.

'Margia's hurt her ankle. She doesn't think that she can walk on it. D'you think she's broken it?' replied Evadne.

Faced with this awful prospect, which hadn't yet occurred to her, Margia briefly lost her battle for self-control, and the tears trickled untrammelled down her face. 'It hurts,' she hiccoughed to herself.

'How can we tell if it's broken?' asked Joey.

'Take her shoes and stockings off and feel, I guess. Come on!'

Poor Margia went even paler at this suggestion of Evadne's. Suppose they felt the end of the broken bone? She felt slightly sick, and turned a delicate shade of green. Joey, meanwhile, was undoing her shoe. Ignoring Margia's grimaces, she eased it off as gently as she could and instructed Margia to undo her stocking, asking, not unreasonably, how they could possibly be expected to tell if the ankle were broken if it was covered in lisle. Neither Joey nor Evadne meant to be rough, but their efforts at Ambulance work were quite painful for poor Margia. They gently poked and prodded at the ankle for about a minute, before Evadne sat back on her heels and surveyed the victim.

'Well, I don't *think* it's broken. I think we should take you up to the school now, and get Matron to strap you up. Come on, get up! And use my hanky,' she added, producing a murky object that had begun its life clean and white, but now, liberally besprinkled with inkspots and grime, was fit only for the ragbag. Margia took one look at the sorry object and decided to use her own, on the grounds that, although it was in a similar state, she at least knew how it had come to be that way. Then Joey and Evadne hauled her up by brute force, and half-carried, half-dragged her to the Chalet.

The Captain, having realised by now that one team was missing, had come to look for them. She took one look at Margia, tearstained, stockingless, and obviously in pain, and called for the Lieutenant. Together, the two women made a queen's chair for the injured girl, and carried her gently into the Headmistress's study, settling her carefully on the sofa. While Miss Bettany waited with her pupil, Miss Maynard departed in search of Matron, while Joey and Evadne stood silently by.

'Joey, please go and fetch a glass of water from Marie for Margia.' Miss Bettany spoke quietly and as Headmistress, rather than sister. 'Evadne,' she continued, as Joey departed on her errand, 'please tell me how Margia came to be in this state. How did she hurt herself? And where is her other shoe and her stocking?'

'On the playing field, still, I guess.'

'You guess? Don't you know for sure?'

'It's—they're on the playing field. Margia fell over, and hurt her ankle. We were checking to see whether she'd broken it or not.'

'Please go and retrieve Margia's shoe and stocking for her. They are of no use to her on the playing field.' Miss Bettany's demeanour was cool, to say the least.

'No, Captain.' Evadne departed as Joey, Miss Maynard and Matron returned. As the two ladies busied themselves with the invalid, Miss Bettany drew her sister gently aside.

'I know that you and Evadne were only trying to help Margia but, in doing so, I can see that you inadvertently caused her unnecessary pain. I shall say no more to you about it, as I can see that you feel very sorry. Do you know what you should have done?'

'Not really.' Joey pushed at the floor with the toe of her shoe, not wishing to meet her sister's gaze.

'One of you should have stayed with her and tried to make her comfortable, while the other went to get help. It would have been easier for Margia if we'd bandaged her on the spot, rather than bring her here to be bandaged. Don't worry!' She smiled down at her sister. 'I have decided that after you have all passed your Tenderfoot tests, the first badge that we shall work on together will be Ambulance, so that you will be ready to take it the moment you have your Second Class badge.'

'I'm glad. It would've been better if we'd known exactly what to do, instead of guessing so much. Is Margia really going to be OK?' asked Jo anxiously.

'Joey, don't worry. She will be quite all right now, and able to join in with the rest of our activities after *Abendessen*.'

'Good-oh!' And together they went outside for the rest of the afternoon's pursuits.

Later that evening, as the new company sat in patrols making flags on a white ground, ten inches deep, with the patrol emblem sewn each side, while the more artistic members began to decorate the covers of the patrol log books with their symbols, Joey slipped across to the Cocks from the Poppies. Margia was laughing and chattering as hard as anyone, her firmly bandaged foot propped up on a stool and almost forgotten about. As she saw Joey approaching, she pushed back her thick curls from her eyes.

'I'm sorry if I hurt you earlier,' began Jo.

'It's OK. Matron's strapped it up ever so tightly, and everything's fine now! I'm not to try and stand on it for a couple of days, and I'm excused practice until the end of the week, 'cos of the pedalling, which won't please Herr Anserl, but I don't really care.' Margia was an extremely gifted pianist, and her piano tutor felt that she should give over all her time to the piano and music generally. She dreamt of becoming a pianiste when she grew up, and was certainly showing promise enough, even at her young age. The school authorities felt, however, that it was important that she should *not* specialise for a few years yet. 'Miss Maynard says that we're all going to do Ambulance badge next, so that we know what to do in a *real* emergency! Guides is absolutely topping!'

'Yes,' smiled Joey, relieved that her sister had been right, and taking advantage of the fact that the prefects were concentrating on their patrol flags. 'Absolutely ripping!'

Chapter VI

A Sunny Afternoon

It was a beautiful summer's afternoon, and the sun's reflections glinted from the Tiern See as it gleamed sapphire-like, framed by the mighty alpine peaks of the Bärenbad Alpe, the Tiernjoch, the Mondescheinspitze and the Bärenkopf. The various members of the Chalet School were enjoying themselves under large Chinese parasols in the school's grounds, while its young Headmistress walked back from visiting 'the apple woman' with her younger sister. Madge and Joey had very little time together during term time, and Joey had seized the opportunity to go walking with her sister that afternoon.

'Madge,' began Joey, as she bit into an enormous apple, 'how long will it be before the San's ready?'

'Oh, at least a year yet, Joey-baba. They've only just begun building it. Jem showed me the building site when I was last up there, and, really, it's still a big hole in the ground.'

'What about your house?'

'Joey,' Madge laughed, her sherry-coloured eyes dancing, 'it's not my house yet. It's Jem's house, and he'll be sharing it with Captain Humphries for a while longer—when he comes back from Russia he'll be Jem's secretary. It's a very large chalet, with plenty of space and a large garden round it. We thought we'd make a rose garden up there, with all the varieties of roses that we had in Devon.'

'Gorgeous!' sighed Jo, who had spent many afternoons reading in the rose garden at Greenacres when they had lived in Devon.

The heavy scent had permeated several books, and, for Jo, *Wuthering Heights* was rose, not heather, scented. 'And where shall the Robin and I sleep? Will we be able to see it?'

'You will both be up near the top, and yes, you'll be able to see the roses from your bedroom window, and smell them too, if Devon was anything to go by. It will be simply beautiful.'

'Is it the house close to Plato's house? How often d'you think we'll see him and Sally-go-round-the-moon in the hols? It must be ever so noisy up there, with all the sawing an' hammering an' so on. D'you think he's getting annoyed and getting into one of his rages?'

'Plato' was the nickname bestowed upon the Chalet School's singing master, one Tristan Denny. He had waxed lyrical on the subject of Plato's Republic when he had first arrived to teach the girls, and the naughty Middles had nicknamed him 'Plato' as a result. His health had deteriorated recently: the vivid pink-and-white skin that added to his unusual looks belied the severity of the illness that had brought him to the Tiern See, and he and his sister, Sarah, had moved further up the alpe on his doctor's orders during the Easter holiday. Now under the direct care of Dr Russell, he was improving, but had not yet returned to teaching the girls.

'Will he be back soon? It's not the same singing songs with Mademoiselle, and we need to practise for the folk festival at the end of the term!'

'Slow down, Joey-baba! You are full of questions today! I'm sure we'll see plenty of the Dennys if they are still living up there by the time we move. And you know full well that won't be for at least a year. The Sanatorium has to be properly established, as well as the Chalet School is now, before Jem and I will marry. Yes, it's very noisy there at the moment, and I'm sure Mr Denny wishes he were elsewhere some days! Jem needs to give the building works a great deal of attention for now.'

'Is that why Jem's not been down to see us this term?' inquired Jo. The previous terms had seen several visits from the young doctor, and not solely when Jo herself, or one of the other pupils of the Chalet School, had been ill.

'Partly. And partly because some of the patients who are up there are very ill, and he needs to look after them.' Madge's brow creased a little at the thought. Madame Pagnol was one of the patients who required Dr Russell's attentions, and the young Headmistress was worried about Madame Pagnol's daughter, Stéphanie. The Chalet School's policy was not to hide the harshness of illness from its pupils, but to help them through the hard times. Since becoming a boarder, Stéphanie had been little more involved in the out-of-school activities of her schoolfellows than she had been as a day girl. Of all the Seniors, she was by far the quietest, and, at Guides, she was noticeably lagging behind the rest of the girls in passing all her Tenderfoot tests.

Kind-hearted Jo checked the diatribe into which she had been about to launch: it was not, after all, Dr Russell's fault that he had not been down to visit them. They walked along the lakeside in silence, eating their apples, until they reached the Chalet School's swimming spot. Jo turned to her sister. She was a perceptive child, but her next question startled Madge even so, coming, as it did, without preamble.

'Is one of them, one of the patients, Stéphanie's mother? Is she as ill as the Robin's mother was? D'you think that's why Stéphanie's not been joining in as much as Aurélie does?'

The Bettanys' mother had died when Joey was still a baby, and, not having known anything but the love of her sister and her sister's twin, Dick, she did not really miss her mother. She had, however, seen how badly the Robin had been affected by her mother's death. Joey remembered vividly how, during the previous term, the girls had been talking of the different dances they could perform and the songs they could sing for their summer folk festival, and the baby of the school had begun singing her mother's lullaby, 'The Red Sarafan'. Only a verse or so in, she had burst into inconsolable sobs, plaintively crying for 'Maman', whom she would never see again.

'Stéphanie's mother is very ill, Joey, and Stéphanie is worried about her, yes. Be kind to her, as I know you always are, but don't fuss over her—just as you were kind to Juliet when her parents died. You know what it's like to be fussed over, and how much you resent it. There's no need for you to broadcast this round the school, and I know that I can rely upon you.' From her earliest age, Jo had been included in all the family's discussions, and her brother and sister knew that she was capable of discretion: this term she had proved this very well by not revealing to her school chums that her sister was going to be married.

Joey swallowed some apple. 'I understand. Like when Grizel's Grannie died, too.'

'Yes, like then.'

The sisters turned in at the school gate, and, pausing briefly to hug her sister, Joey raced off to find her coterie, who were sprawling at the edge of the playing field, their minds full of Tenderfoot tests, with the Robin and some of the rest of the Juniors practising plaiting each other's hair nearby.

'I do not think that I shall ever know how to tie these knots!' sighed Simone, her neat little head looking, for once, almost as golliwog-like as Joey's. 'When I think that I have learnt one, I then have to learn another, and then I get verrry confused.' In her irritation, she rolled her 'r's in a thoroughly French manner.

'Mmm,' replied Joey, somewhat indistinctly, since she was engaged in finally demolishing the remnants of her apple. She swallowed, and continued. 'It's the reef knot and the sheet-bend that confuse me. They're so entirely similar!'

'And then, for Second Class, we have to know those and more!' sighed Frieda, looking up from her diagram of the Union Jack, and wishing that it flew from the Chalet School's roof, so that she would be constantly reminded of the correct way to fly it.

'But just think,' interjected Joey, 'what we can do after that! There's all the different Guide badges. Sir Robert Baden-Powell says he always feels more pally towards a Guide with badges on her right arm, you know, the ones which show the sort of Guide you are. I want to do Book Lover, and Authoress, and we can *all* do Interpreter, an' probably Musician too. You can play your harp, Frieda, and I'll sing with you!'

'Me, I wish to do Needlework badge,' said the Robin at this point. 'I can sew almost as well as you, now, Zoë!'

Joey laughed. Her sewing was appalling, particularly compared with that of the continental girls of the school. It really was not difficult for the Robin to be her equal as a needlewoman.

'Yes, Herzliebchen, you can sew very well already, and you are much neater than I am. But you have to be a First Class Brownie before you can work for badges, so you will have plenty of time to get even better. Soon you'll be as good as Mademoiselle at sewing!'

'I too would like to try for Needlewoman,' announced Frieda. 'What is involved?'

Evadne made a dive for her copy of *Girl Guide Badges and How to Win Them*, and found the page.

'"A Guide must show a knowledge of cutting out simple garments in cotton and woollen materials from pattern given at examination—" so that means that we need to practise first. "Patching in various materials and darning stockings." Well, we get plenty of practice at that!' Indeed, Evadne invariably had to darn her stockings once a week. '"Must make entirely by herself and bring to the examination:– (a) A blouse or baby's frock, or equivalent garment, sleeves to be inset; (b) a pair of knickers (one of these may be made by machine if desired)." Well, that's no help, as we don't have a machine.' She took a deep breath and read the last of the requirements. '"At the examination, must make buttonholes and set gathers into a band,"' she concluded. 'That sounds like a *lot* of work. I don't think I'll be in any hurry to try for that one. I fancy Electrician myself. That sounds pie. I'd like to try for Dairymaid too, but I don't know where we'd find a chicken to pluck! I'm sure Pa could get us several if any of you want to have a go with me, though.'

'Eaugh!' cried Simone. 'That sounds most revolting!'

'Still, even if you don't do Needlewoman ever, you've still got to make something for Second Class, and do almost the entire badge *anyhow* for First Class. You'll have to learn how to sew somehow, Evvy!' This was Margia, in whose slim pianist's fingers a needle looked far more at home than it ever would in Evadne's stubby, square hands. 'We'll help you as much as we can—"A Guide's Duty is to be Useful and to Help Others. A Guide is a Friend to All"!' she quoted.

Evadne grimaced at her, and received a gentle punch on the arm in return.

'Now, now! Children! Do play nicely!' Grizel had wandered over from the tree where she had been sitting with the Seniors, debating the possibility of cricket and tennis matches that term; while the Middles were completely obsessed by Guides, the Seniors retained rather more *sang froid* with regard to their new hobby, particularly since one or two of their number had already been Guides. 'What are you doing to Evvy, that she seems to be moved to such violence towards you?' Although not a prefect, Grizel frequently behaved as though she were, justifying her actions to herself by the dignity conferred on her due to her position as Games Captain. 'Perhaps you should do some fielding practice, since you seem to have more than enough energy for your current pursuits?'

'Cricket practice? What on earth for? It's not as if we had any opponents!' Joey did not share Grizel's all-consuming passion for games, although she was as keen as anyone else when not being dictated to. Level-headed as a rule, she inevitably found Grizel somewhat overbearing in her attitude to games, and was often unable to stop herself replying to the elder girl in a rude manner. 'Find us some challengers, and then, perhaps, we'll consider extra practices, 'cos then we'll have something to work towards!'

It was an unfortunate response, as Grizel felt their lack of opponents keenly; and she thus allowed herself to become ruffled by Joey's taunt.

'If *that's* your attitude, then I see no hope for you. You should be ready to play any opponent at a moment's notice! Who knows *whom* I might be able to challenge, tomorrow, even!' And off she stalked, determined to find *someone* against whom to play a cricket match, even if it turned out to be a scratch team of lady walkers staying at one of the nearby hotels.

'Hmm. Isn't a Guide supposed to be courteous?' remarked Joey. 'But then, I s'pose I was about as bad as her, and if she's the kettle, then I'm the pot!'

'The "pot"?' queried Frieda. A year at the English school had improved her English a great deal, but Joey's colloquial epithets were still occasionally beyond her.

'It's an expression. "The pot calling the kettle black" means that you, as the pot, are complaining about the kettle, the other person, but that you are really as bad as they,' Joey explained. 'Before we had stoves, the pot and the kettle used to sit on an open fire, and both would get burnt black by the flames,' she wound up, in her normal lucid manner.

'I see,' replied Frieda, who didn't really, and resolved to ask Madame for an explanation.

Meanwhile, Miss Bettany had convened a staff meeting inside the school. There were several pressing matters to discuss, not least the girls' all-encompassing enthusiasm for Guiding. All the staff worried that their pupils' work was beginning to deteriorate, and that the girls were inclined to think about their Guiding tests during their lessons, rather than their school work.

'Now, ladies,' began Miss Bettany, 'it is such a glorious day that I am sure you would all prefer to relax outside. However, we do need to make some plans, and to debate what we shall do at half term. The first item on the agenda is Guides. While I am sure that we are all pleased that the new company has been such a success, we need to make sure that nothing else falls behind, and we must remain vigilant!'

'Absolutely!' Miss Maynard agreed. 'Some days, the only way to engage the girls' attention seems to be to relate the mathematical problems to Guiding, and, really, that only serves to reinforce the idea that Guides could, and should, occupy their minds all the time. They are better than they were at the beginning of term, but there is still much room for improvement.'

'I'm still a little worried about the Middles.' Miss Carthew's voice showed her concern. 'As Maynie says, it seems that the only way to get anyone to learn anything at the moment is to relate it to some aspect of Guiding. And while it's perfectly sensible to work in observation skills with geography—and there's a certain amount you can do, as you said, with mathematics—apart from the legends of the Crosses of the Union Jack, it really is entirely impossible to tie up European history with Guiding; it's such a new movement!'

'It's harder than you'd imagine with mathematics,' replied Miss Maynard to her colleague's diatribe. 'Agreed, when setting problems, one can substitute Guides for workmen; and there's a fair amount in the handbook about triangulation which is easy to work in; but that's all, and really, their minds seem completely preoccupied with Guides!'

'Is there nothing we can do? At this rate, I shall have to rewrite the exams I've set for the end of the term; we simply won't have covered the necessary ground!' and Miss Carthew sat back with a sigh. 'Are all Guides as bad as this?'

'Och, I don't think you can say that they're bad, exactly,' interjected Matron in her soft, lilting voice, 'just very keen. Some of them really can't wait to begin working on badges, and at every turn I seem to be ambushed by girls demanding to know the correct way to treat a sprained ankle, or to check the knots on the latest limb they've bandaged!' She smiled. 'If not that, then they keep asking me how I starch my cap and how to get stains out of handkerchiefs!'

'Perhaps it will all blow over when it gets too warm to concentrate their energies on Guiding all the time,' suggested Miss Durrant. 'The Juniors seem to be less gripped by the fever; although this may be because the Brownie tests are simpler. Even so, perhaps a few remarks about keeping the spirit of the Guide Laws might help; it may not have occurred to some of the more enthusiastic members of the company that their duty lies as much in school work as it does in Guiding.'

'I think that would be a good idea. Otherwise, I fear, we shall have to ask you to postpone their meetings for a little while, Madame, in order to give them the opportunity to concentrate on school matters. And that,' said Mademoiselle, 'is not something that I should like to do.'

'I quite agree!' replied Miss Maynard. 'I shall make sure that we mention this at the next meeting when we enrol them. We need to have a short break from all types of test work before they begin their Second Class, and any Guide badges they might want to try, anyhow; and as far as I'm concerned, this settles it.'

'So you think that the best way to counteract the unwanted side-effects of Guides is to distract them completely?' asked Miss Bettany, who had been listening to her colleagues' conversation with great interest.

'Perhaps, yes,' replied Mademoiselle. 'I think that it is simply a matter of breaking the connection briefly, and letting them remember that there are things other than Guide tests with which they should be concerning themselves.'

'It is half term the week after next, and we shall be visiting the Sonnalpe. There will be the opportunity to make a break there, for a while. At the same time, if we go up there on a Saturday they will expect some sort of Guide meeting.'

'It doesn't need to be on a Saturday, though, does it, if it's at half term? Although the walk up would be a lovely opportunity to play a tracking game,' Miss Maynard interjected. 'There's that big meadow with the long grass, which would be very good for hiding objects that needed to be found.'

Miss Bettany considered for a moment. 'Ye-es. I can see that would be a wonderful opportunity. We'll need to do something to counterbalance the Guiding aspect, though.'

'How about natural pictures?' Miss Carthew suggested. 'We used to make those when I was a girl. They are very simple, but quite effective. The girls can collect leaves, flowers, feathers, stones and so forth on their way up to the Sonnalpe, or on the way back down, and then, when we are back, we could have a special Hobbies Club where they arrange their finds into pictures. It works especially well if they are arranged in shoeboxes standing on their sides, although we would be hard pressed to get enough shoeboxes for our numbers in the space of a week.'

'Oh, those would be pretty. And, instead of the shoeboxes,

we could make our own boxes out of cardboard. I am sure I can arrange for a supply to be sent up from Innsbruck this week,' Miss Bettany replied. 'It is always a useful skill to be able to make one's own boxes out of card, too. Sometimes there simply isn't a box that's the right size for a parcel. Good. I am glad to think that we may be able to solve that problem. I also think that Miss Maynard is right: please don't encourage the girls by pandering to their desires in lessons!

'Next, we should consider the folk festival. Joey mentioned this to me today, which reminded me that we have not decided exactly who will be doing what. Mr Denny has furnished me with a list of suitable songs, and, Miss Durrant, I believe you have a list of dances, as well as the nursery rhymes for the Juniors?'

'Yes.' Miss Durrant handed over a sheet of paper. 'Of course, the dancing all rather depends on how the Seniors get on with morris dancing. I think they will be able to perform "Laudnum Bunches" well enough, but I shall not be sure until the week before. Will that be too late for programmes?'

'No, not at all,' replied Miss Bettany. 'Rather than print lots of programmes, I thought we could set up one of the blackboards on an easel next to where we perform, and write the programme on that. It would be a little like the music hall, I admit, but much easier to manage.'

'That is a wonderful idea, *ma chérie*!' enthused Mademoiselle. 'Perhaps we could ask Wanda to decorate the edge of the board with pictures of roses, in chalk, similar to the flowers she paints on to her china?' Wanda von Eschenau was very skilled in painting patterns on to china during the school's Hobbies Club, and she had completed almost a whole coffee service in the last year.

Miss Bettany made a note on her agenda sheet. 'I shall ask her after the meeting. I am sure she would very much like to do that for us. But back to the songs and dances. Mademoiselle, do you have the songs and dances for the French girls?'

'*Oui*, Miss Durrant and I have been helping them learn the Breton dances, such as the fisherwomen dance, and they are doing very well.' She too handed over her sheet of paper. 'Simone, Renée, Stéphanie, Aurélie, Suzanne, Yvette and Honorine will dance together, and I know that Bianca and Luigia wish to dance a tarantella, as they have asked me to play the piano to accompany them.'

'Well, that should scare off any passing tarantulas all right!' remarked Matron with a twinkle. 'Oh, but you don't get them in these parts, do you?'

'No, I think they're found more in the southern Mediterranean, aren't they?' responded Madge, laughing. 'I'm fairly sure there are no venomous spiders in the Tyrol. There are some snakes in the area—in fact, Amy saw one last year—but they are very few in number, and most of them are harmless green grass snakes. We have not yet seen a viper, and I hope that we never shall!'

'Now, who else do we need to consider?'

'The Norwegian girls,' said Miss Maynard. 'Also Cyrilla, and Evadne, and the Robin.'

'All the Juniors, I believe, will be singing "The Red Sarafan", although not in the original Russian. Captain Humphries sent me a translation some months ago, and Mr Denny has taught this to the girls.' Miss Bettany glanced at her notes before continuing. 'The Eriksen girls have asked if they could write to get the music for a particular song they know, and we are trying to obtain that, while Cyrilla wishes to dance a Mazurka.'

'And Evadne?'

'An Appalachian song, I gather, from that book you gave Joey last year,' Miss Bettany replied.

'Oh, Grizel won't like that!' Miss Maynard replied. 'She

absolutely hated the way Joey *would* sing them in season and out.'

'Fortunately Evadne is a little more circumspect than Joey, and has been practising the songs well away from Grizel,' Miss Durrant replied.

'Evadne? Circumspect?' Miss Carthew looked a little doubtful.

'Well, she heard all about Grizel's feelings on the subject from Joey, so she has been making sure that Grizel is well out of earshot before she practises.'

'Now, is there any other business?' Miss Bettany asked, steering the meeting back on course. 'No? In which case, I think we should go and enjoy the sunshine.'

This pronouncement came not a moment too soon, as one of the Juniors came knocking at the door of the staffroom, to request that Matron come 'as quickly as possible, and even quicker than that' since Amy Stevens had fallen over and grazed her knee, and was wailing piteously a few hundred yards away. Matron Wilson bade farewell to her colleagues, and picking up the small First Aid kit she invariably carried with her, hurried over to soothe Amy's hurt.

Chapter VII

Triumph and Disaster

As half term approached Miss Bettany congratulated herself on her plan to take the School on an excursion to one of the higher alpes. The weather was proving to be exceptionally good, and there had been no thunderstorms yet. She remembered only too well an occasion the previous summer when a thunderstorm had taken them by surprise and they had been forced to take shelter in a goatherd's hut on the Mondscheinspitze. Warned by this experience, she had prudently decided that it would be as well to take the opportunity for a day out well before the storms were due. It would also, as Miss Maynard had suggested, be an excellent opportunity for the girls to practise stalking positions and tracking, and she hoped that giving them a morning's worth of Guiding activities directly after their enrolment ceremony would help them continue to settle down to school work during school hours.

On the Saturday of the enrolment the entire school was thoroughly overexcited and almost feverish with anticipation. In the big Yellow dormitory Jo was as usual the first awake, and the moment the rising bell rang she was on her feet and hurrying across to the window.

'Hurry up and get up, you folks! It's a simply *ripping* day! The quicker we get up, the sooner we can enjoy it. Oh, do come along! Who's on first bath?' And she dashed over to the list, not noticing that her yellow dressing gown cord, trailing in its usual manner from only one of the belt loops, had wrapped itself round one of the legs of the chair in her cubicle. She was momentarily brought up short as it tautened, and turned to look at it in consternation.

'Dratted thing!' she remarked, before giving the cord a sharp tug, intending to free it from the chair. Instead the chair fell over with a resounding crash—bringing Juliet, the dormitory head, to her cubicle post haste to see what on earth had happened. There she found Joey on hands and knees, hair in more than its usual disarray, attempting to disentangle her cord from the chair. Her clothes were scattered over the floor and the chair itself had definitely seen better days.

'What *are* you doing?' she inquired. 'More to the point, what *were* you doing to get into such a state in the first place? If you're not careful, Matron will be in to find out what's going on; and Gisela and Bernhilda are overhead, as well. Are you hurt?'

'No, no, I'm fine, but I'm afraid the chair's a bit dented!' And with a final violent pull, she managed to disentangle herself. 'Who's first for the bathroom, anyhow?'

'You, so you'd better hurry. I'll pick this lot up, otherwise you'll never be ready in time. It's all right, I don't think you'll have to pay for extra laundry. Now scoot!'

'Thanks awfully, Juliet, you are a brick! I'd better run!' Joey suited the action to the word and headed towards the bathroom, while Juliet set the misused furniture to rights and rearranged the clothes. Then she darted to her own cubicle to continue stripping her bed, gesticulating wildly at the rest of the dormitory to mind its own business and go on with getting up. Joey's mishap had had one positive result: even Evadne was out of bed, and she was as fond of her bed as a snail is of its shell.

Frühstück passed almost without incident, apart from a small upset perpetrated by Ingeborg Eriksen, a Norwegian child, who, in making a long arm for the honey, knocked the nearest jug of milk over her elder sister Thyra. The resulting cacophony had to be heard to be believed, with a Babel of exclamations in all languages issuing from the excited children. Miss Durrant chose the newest Junior, Honorine Drouin, from the plethora of Brownies who volunteered for the job, to go scurrying for a cloth with which to wipe the table and floor, and then turned her attention to calming the rest of the crowd.

'Do stop howling, Thyra! You're not made of sugar, and I'm sure you won't melt for a bit of milk! Was that really clean on today? Well, you'll just have to change your clothes and wear yesterday's frock until that dress has been sent to the laundry. Now,' fishing her handkerchief out of her pocket, and mopping Thyra's face, 'blow your nose, and we'll have no more tears. Thank you, Honorine—oh!'

At this moment Honorine came rushing up, proffering a cloth, and slipped on the not inconsiderable puddle of milk that had been slowly spreading on the floor. Down she fell with a bang that rivalled Joey's efforts in the dormitory, and promptly burst into tears. The ensuing commotion brought Miss Bettany over from the staff table, followed closely by Mademoiselle, and together the three ladies managed to calm the overwrought Juniors, ascertaining that Honorine was not badly hurt, just a little jolted; and calm reigned once again.

The next upset came as the Seniors were settling down to do their mending. Bernhilda and the day girls were just joining the boarders in the large formroom used by the Seniors for sewing. The usual babble of greetings filled the air as they were reunited, and the boarders related the incidents that had enlivened breakfast. All but Stéphanie had passed their Tenderfoot tests the previous week, and were thus due to be enrolled, and the girls had turned their attention back to other matters, to the relief of all concerned. Grizel in particular was pleased that she could give more time to games: although the novelty of Guides was yet to wear off, she was beginning to realise that she was neglecting her responsibilities. While she was not yet a prefect, she took her duties very seriously and dreamed that, one day, she might be able to become a Games Mistress at a big girls' school. Her parents had other plans for her, but this did not stop her daydreams.

'Perhaps now we're about to be enrolled, they'll start to concentrate on sports a little more. In fact, I've got some ideas for matches for us. You know that party of schoolboys from one of the big London schools, who are staying at the Post?' Flushed with enthusiasm, Grizel had not yet begun her mending.

'Yes,' answered Gisela.

'I thought we'd challenge them to a cricket match. It would be a terrific thing if we could beat them! Just think how bucked everyone would be!'

'But do you think that Madame would allow it? It is a very different thing, for us, to challenge a boys' school,' replied Bernhilda.

'Mm-mm, but it's the only chance I can see of us actually being able to play any matches this term. We might take on some of the hotel people at tennis; but that would be it. Got any white wool? I've got a hole in my sleeve I must mend before Matron sees it!'

'However did you manage to tear it so badly?' asked Mary, rummaging in her work basket.

'Caught it on a branch last week, when we were tracking,' replied Grizel, as Mary threw the ball across to her. It landed between Grizel's seat and that of Gisela, and both leant down to reach for it simultaneously, banging their heads together with a dull 'thunk'.

'Owww!' moaned Grizel. 'I've bitten my tongue!'

'*Ach!*' cried Gisela, straightening gingerly. '*Mein Kopf!* Oooh-ooh! I just saw stars!'

'Perhaps we should take you to Matron,' suggested Rosalie. 'You've gone very pale. Oh, put your head between your knees, do, before you faint!' Indeed, Gisela had gone as white as a ghost with the shock. 'Mary, you go and find Matron, while I look after Gisela. How do you feel, Grizel?'

'Not too bad, thanks,' replied Grizel. 'Think my head's harder than Gisela's. Can you see any blood? My tongue feels awfully odd,' and she stuck out her tongue for inspection.

'No, no blood. But I wouldn't advise jumping around like that, and I think you'd benefit from a glass of water if your tongue hurts. Do sit down quietly, there's a dear.'

Matron soon arrived, and examined the two girls.

'Well, I don't think either of you has suffered a concussion, but you should sit quietly, and Gisela's going to need a cold compress for that bump. Och, yes,' in answer to an anxious query from Mary, 'they'll both be able to make their promises at the ceremony; but there is to be no drilling for either of you, and you are to sit quietly all afternoon, doing as little as possible. And that means no reading!' Matron's brown eyes twinkled. 'You may join the Juniors, and listen to their story if you like, though. I believe they're having *Wind in the Willows* today, which is one of my favourites.'

She straightened up from ministering to her patients, and left to obtain a compress. Gisela's brow was already beginning to swell from the impact of Grizel's head, and it was important to apply the remedy as soon as possible, in order to keep the size of the lump down.

*

Solemnly, Stéphanie stood and watched as Joey Bettany made her promise. Madame's small sister's face was aglow with pride as she repeated the words that would allow her to become a Girl Guide. Her Patrol Leader, Juliet, stood a little behind her to her left, Captain and Lieutenant faced her, and the rest of the company surrounded them in a perfect horseshoe. All that was missing was a company flag—the company was so new that they did not yet have one.

The morning's mishaps were all but forgotten as the girls were caught up in the simple ceremony. Each in turn had been brought by her Patrol Leader to stand before her Captain, Miss Bettany, and had made her promise standing proud and erect in the sunshine.

Stéphanie felt a little forlorn. She had not yet completed her Tenderfoot tests because she had been needed by her mother on more than one Saturday morning. Even if she had been ready, her mother would not have been able to be there to watch her make her promise as a Guide. Madame Pagnol was increasingly weak, and could do little more than listen to her daughter telling her news on her visits. She certainly would not have been well enough to make the trip down from the Sonnalpe, even for so important an occasion in her daughter's life. Stéphanie quickly swallowed the lump in her throat, and turned her attention to Simone, who, accompanied by Grizel, was marching smartly to stand before Captain and Lieutenant.

The enrolment ceremony thus passed without incident, which was something of a relief to both the Captain and Lieutenant, given the upsets that had gone before. The parents of all the day girls had been invited to watch, and to have *Mittagessen* with the School afterwards. They were greatly impressed by the smart appearance of the Guides, in their navy jumpers and skirts and yellow ties; as well as by the neatness of their drill and their knowledge not only of the British flag, but of the flags of all the countries represented by the School. In fact it had proved so onerous for the girls to learn all this information, as the School contained girls of seven different nationalities, that Miss Bettany and Miss Maynard had decided that in future, since they were an English Guide company, they would concentrate on the Union Jack.

Each patrol had given a short display, demonstrating their knowledge of the flags and the stories behind them, as well as what they had learned about their patrol flowers and birds. The Brownies had had their turn, too, and had demonstrated their prowess at sending messages by semaphore. Although the watching parents could not understand the messages, it was obvious from the precise positioning of their flags that the girls had been very well taught.

'I believe,' remarked Herr Mensch, 'that the English Guides are a very useful institution. They are teaching our girls a sense of oneness, and, from what Frieda and Bernhilda have told us, the skills that they learn will be useful throughout their lives, *nicht wahr?*'

'Yes, indeed, Herr Mensch. Guiding is more, however, than just a way to learn useful skills,' replied Miss Bettany. 'It also teaches teamwork, and how to act in an emergency, and how to be helpful generally.'

'A fine organisation, indeed,' he replied. 'And you, *meine liebe* Robin, are you to be a Guide, too?'

'Not yet, Onkel Riese. But next week, *I* shall be a *proper* Brownie,' she said impressively. 'Would you like to zoin too?' The Robin still muddled her 'z's and 'j's in a way that reminded one that her first language was French.

'If Madame will allow me, I shall be honoured!' He beamed down at the cherubic child, whose round face and dark curls so closely resembled those of the pretty sister who had died before he was born, but who still occupied a place in the family's hearts.

Miss Bettany laughed.

'You are very welcome indeed to join us again, if you wish! But I fear that you are a little too old to be a Brownie, as the Robin suggests. Would you like some more coffee?'

'Thank you, Madame.' Herr Mensch held out his cup, and the conversation soon turned to other matters.

There was every expectation among the Staff and pupils that the rest of the day would pass without incident, despite the run of accidents that morning. Indeed, some of the more superstitious members of the school felt that, since bad luck always comes in threes, there would certainly be no more. Alas, this was not to be the case. Although the afternoon itself was peaceful, with Grizel and Gisela both joining the 'babies' for their story, an event which pleased the little ones greatly, the evening saw a mishap which eclipsed all that had gone before.

At around a quarter to eighteen, as everyone was changing for *Abendessen*, an appalling shriek issued from the kitchen, where Marie and Luise Pfeiffen were putting the final touches to the meal, chattering with their cousin Rosa about the day's activities, and wishing that they too might become members of the 1st Tiern See Guide Company. A loud crash followed almost immediately.

Within moments, those members of staff who were accommodated in the main building had assembled at the door to the kitchen. There, Luise was sitting weeping with blood oozing from between her fingers, her hands clutched against her chest.

'*Luise, was ist los? Was ist geschehen?*' asked Miss Bettany, hurrying over to the girl. 'What happened? Let me see!'

Meanwhile, Miss Maynard was bent over Marie, who had fainted at the sight of the blood, and was now lying among the shredded lettuce that had been intended as part of the School's supper. She turned to Rosa, who was crying piteously, her apron clutched to her face.

'Find a stool for me to rest Marie's legs on, please, Rosa. She has only fainted, and will soon be well; but her legs should be raised so that the blood can flow back to her brain. Come, there is nothing to cry over. I shall go and look for brandy to rouse her.'

Rosa obeyed, and Miss Maynard departed in search of the draught.

'Matron,' said Miss Bettany, as they applied a tourniquet to Luise's arm, to quell the flow of blood, 'do you think that Luise will need stitches? It is a very nasty cut, quite deep.'

Once the bleeding lessened, Matron was able to examine the poor hand more closely. It was indeed a bad cut, as the knives that the kitchen staff at the Chalet used were kept extremely sharp by one of Marie and Luise's younger brothers, Hansi. However, it was also an extremely clean cut, and this told in Luise's favour.

'Yes, I think she might. Miss Carthew, could you go and telephone for Dr Erckhardt? I believe Herr Braun said that he was at the Kron Prinz Karl this afternoon. It will take too long for Dr Russell to come down from the Sonnalpe to be of any help to us.'

As Miss Carthew departed, Miss Maynard returned with the brandy. Carefully she moistened Marie's lips, and was rewarded by a fluttering of the eyelids and a gentle moan. Marie gradually revived, and began to try to sit up.

'Slowly, Marie. You will feel better soon, but if you sit up too quickly, you will just faint again,' she said, in German. 'Luise has cut her hand, but she will be well again soon. When you are ready, we shall help you to cut some more lettuce for supper.'

'*Danke schön, mein Fräulein*,' replied the grateful Marie, pleased that her mistress had taken charge, and her sister was being well cared for. She was always grateful for the kindness of her employer, and frequently thanked her Maker for this blessing.

The girls were beginning to make their way to the Speisesaal, wondering why the bell had not yet rung, and speculating as to the cause. Several of the Seniors, realising the extent of the disaster, offered to help cut more lettuce, while Matron and Miss Carthew took the unfortunate Luise, her wound tightly bound, up to the san to await Dr Erckhardt's ministrations.

Over a somewhat late supper, the girls sympathised with Luise's plight. She was a firm favourite with them, and they were sorry that she had been hurt while preparing their meal.

'Just think, though,' Margia remarked. 'We could have helped to bandage her up if we'd been on the spot. That would have been such good Ambulance practice!'

Chapter VIII

AN EXPEDITION

FOLLOWING this drama-filled day, the girls of the Chalet School were justly tired, and they all slept extremely well that night. A typically quiet Sunday followed, with the Roman Catholic girls able to attend a service of High Mass: this could only happen once in every three weeks, as the priest who looked after the little whitewashed chapel near the Kron Prinz Karl also had to minister to Torteswald and Buchau. The Protestant girls, who were in the minority, had a little service of their own with Miss Bettany and the other English mistresses in one of the schoolrooms. They lazed around during the afternoon, reading books or chattering peacefully, and, as usual, had their quiet talks with Mademoiselle or Madame in the evening.

They all awoke refreshed early the next morning, and, apart from the Juniors over at Le Petit Chalet, immediately dressed in their climbing gear. They were to go on a long hike up to the Sonnalpe, with plenty of tracking games on the way to encourage their observation skills.

Naturally, the Middles were all agog as to the type of games that would be played and talked of nothing else during *Frühstück* and on their way to Prayers. There the discussion halted, as the Catholic girls made their devotions with Mademoiselle La Pâttre in the larger Speisesaal, while the Protestants had Prayers with Madame in one of the classrooms.

'Are we going to have a picnic for elevenses on the way up? Remember how hungry we got last year, climbing up to the

Bärenbad Alpe?' asked Margia, as the Protestant girls rejoined the Catholics in the Speisesaal after Prayers.

'No, there won't be time to stop and wait around,' replied Juliet, 'if we want to reach the Sonnalpe for lunch. But if I were you, I'd take some chocolate—that is if you've got any, and we'll be able to stop and buy some apples from the apple woman, so take some cash with you. Assuming that it hasn't *all* gone on fines this week.' For earlier in the week, Juliet had caught Margia in the act of describing her piano tutor, Herr Anserl, as 'the vilest, most bossiest, rotten old thing' after a particularly fraught lesson one afternoon. Herr Anserl was extremely short tempered, and had a reputation for being a hard taskmaster and remorselessly critical if his pupils failed to attain the standards he expected. Although Margia had tried her hardest, she had failed to please the irascible master, and she had vented her feelings to Evadne in the garden after her lesson. As a result, most of that week's pocket money had gone into the fines box and Margia was left with the bare minimum required for necessities such as stamps.

Satisfied with Juliet's answer, Margia went to announce the news to her own particular coterie; if she didn't have money for apples, one of her friends almost certainly would, and would buy one for her, as lending was strictly forbidden.

It was not long before the Middles and Seniors were assembled at the front of the Chalet; the Juniors were to have their own walk up to the Bärenbad Alpe, and go to the Gasthaus on the Alm for bread and butter, followed by wild strawberries with saucers of thick, yellow cream. Assembled in their climbing gear of short brown tweed skirt, with matching beret, white jumper and stout boots, they made a trig and trim set, worthy of any Guide company. The mistresses were similarly attired, in jumpers of brighter hue, as was Matron. Rufus was joining them for the trip, and romped around joyously as his young mistress tried to attach his lead.

'Rufus. Sit! Sit! I can't get your lead on if you don't keep still. Oh, *sit*!' Joey was getting increasingly exasperated as the over-excited dog bounded from Middle to Middle, greeting all his friends, as he hadn't seen the girls since the previous day, and he needed to make sure that everyone was in good health. 'Simone, can you help me hold on to him, please. I shall never get the lead on to him otherwise, and I don't want to have to leave him behind!'

Together, the two girls were quickly able to calm the dog, and persuade him to sit, although his great tail swept the grass incessantly while they secured his lead to his collar. Simone adored Joey, and thus she adored Rufus; otherwise, she might well have been scared of the great St Bernard dog, who was still little more than a puppy in age, and certainly believed himself to be a puppy still.

'Thanks, Simone. That definitely helped. Now, Rufus, you are going to behave today!' Joey waggled a finger at him, and he looked at her with a serious air, before bouncing up again and pulling at his lead.

'Matron looks verrry pretty, does she not?' murmured Simone to Joey, and, indeed, against her soft blue jumper, Matron's eyes took on a deeper shade of brown, while the gentle breeze whipped roses into her cheeks. Without the stiff starch of her everyday garb, she looked barely older than Gisela, and certainly not old enough to be Matron of such a large school.

'And so does Ma—my sister,' replied Joey as she struggled to control her boisterous pet. 'Rufus! Sit! Russet really is her colour! Oh, good boy!' This last as Rufus finally deigned to sit still and wait patiently while the girls organised themselves.

'Now, do we have everything?' asked Miss Bettany, when they were quiet. 'Who has the lemonade? We don't want to leave it behind. You, Bette? Well done. And who has the fruit? And the sandwiches? And the parasols? Good. I'm sure I don't really need to remind you to take turn about in carrying the baskets: no-one should carry them for the whole journey up or down! Ready, girls?'

'Yes, Madame!' chorused the girls.

'Then off we go!'

They set off across the playing field, through the wicket gate and a meadow filled with June flowers, and caught the ferry from Briesau to Seespitz. It was still early enough for the ferry to be quiet and empty of tourists, and the girls drank in the peaceful blue beauty of the lake. They spoke in undertones, moved by the Tiern See's unearthly loveliness. Arriving in Seespitz, they collected Frieda and Bernhilda, and paused at the edge of the water meadows that lead to Maurach.

'You may have noticed, girls,' Miss Bettany began, 'that Miss Maynard and Matron went on ahead of the rest of us. This is because they have been preparing two tracking games for you. The first we shall play across the meadows. Many of you have read *Daddy-Long-Legs* or *The Railway Children*, and will remember the games of "Hare and Hounds" in those books.'

'Oh, yes, Miss Bettany!' piped up Margia. 'And how, in *Daddy-Long-Legs*, the hares tried to trick the hounds by laying the paper trail to look as though it was going through a barn! I liked that part.'

'Well,' continued the Headmistress, smiling at Margia's enthusiasm, 'we are going to play a variation of "Hare and Hounds" called "The Jewel Thief". Now, listen carefully, girls, as I shall not explain this a second time. Miss Maynard and Matron are jewel thieves who are trying to escape from you, their pursuers. They have dropped their jewels as they go. We have made the jewels out of coloured paper, and each different colour and shape represents a different jewel. White diamonds are diamonds, white circles are pearls, blue ones are sapphires, green ones emeralds, red ones rubies and orange ones are jacinths. Each jewel will earn you a certain number of points for your patrol: a pearl counts five, a sapphire four, a ruby three, a jacinth two, an emerald one, while a diamond counts ten. There are only four diamonds. The patrol which gets the most points will win the game.

'Now, please divide into your patrols. Keep your eyes peeled, and I will see you on the other side of the meadow. Ready? On the count of three. One, two, three!' and Miss Bettany blew her whistle to signal the beginning of the game.

The patrols spread out across the grass, chattering quietly. Almost immediately, Evadne swooped on a piece of red paper.

'Gee, I've found a "ruby"! I never thought I'd be the first one to find something! Guess Guides is doing me some good. Here!' and she passed the scrap of paper to Juliet, the Patrol Leader of the Poppies, for safe keeping.

Bianca di Ferrara was the next to find a scrap, this time orange, and quietly passed the 'jacinth' to the Cocks' Patrol Leader, Gertrud. After that, exclamations of delight came thick and fast, as the girls found more of the precious stones, and stored them up. It was not easy to spot them in the long grass of the water meadow, particularly since the flowers mirrored the colours of the jewels. Matron and Miss Maynard had done their job well, and had spaced the jewels out just far enough to allow each girl a chance of finding at least one of their own.

'Look, Simone!' cried Frieda, as they walked with their patrol, the Cornflowers, 'I think I can see a diamond!'

They plunged towards it, and narrowly missed hitting their heads together as Simone bent to look more closely at the paper shape while Frieda plucked it from the grass. 'Here, Grizel, we've got a diamond! Look!'

Grizel hurried over. 'Well done! If we can find another, then we're bound to win the game. Keep your eyes open, and look wide, Cornflowers!'

She tucked the little diamond safely into her pocket, and they all moved forward, eyes anxiously scanning the field. A yelp to their right announced that Joey had also found a diamond, and then a squawk from just behind heralded the news that Paula von Rothenfels had found the third for the Swallow patrol. Grizel gritted her teeth. She was determined that no other patrol should find the last diamond, and her determination was intensified by the knowledge that the Cornflowers lacked a patrol member, as Stéphanie was up on the Sonnalpe with her mother.

'Buck up, girls!' she cried. 'There's one more to find, and we're going to find it. Oh!'

She stopped short, as she glimpsed the last diamond peeking out from behind a blade of grass, and started towards it. Just as she was drawing near, Margia Stevens swooped down on it and snatched it up, crying to her Patrol Leader:

'I've found it! Gertrud, I've found a diamond!'

Grizel had perforce to bite her tongue and congratulate the winners, as they reached the other side of the meadow and Miss Bettany counted up the jewels each had found. The Cock patrol came in first, with forty-five points, the Cornflowers were second with forty-two, the Swallows third with thirty-eight, and the Poppies came last, despite their good start, with thirty-seven points. That diamond would have made a world of difference to their finishing position, but she had to remember to keep the Guide Laws, and be cheerful and graceful in defeat. Forcing back the bile that had risen in her throat at being beaten by one of the Middles, she managed to smile and agree that it had been a good game and great fun.

Miss Bettany had noticed Grizel's behaviour during the game. The School's Games Captain was known for her hard character and short temper, as well as her deep hatred of failing at anything she tried, and the young Headmistress was pleased to see that, this time at least, she had swallowed her disappointment and was behaving in a kind and courteous manner. Grizel had been so keen to become a Guide, and her enthusiasm was, for the moment, paying dividends.

At length they reached the narrow path that would take them up to the Sonnalpe. Although the walk began gently, passing through more meadows and thence into the shady pine forest, the temperature was already beginning to rise, making the girls eager to reach the cover of the trees. It would be worse as the day warmed and the path steepened.

'I reckon it'll be full of midges and other flying things that bite, though,' remarked Evadne.

'But the air is so delicious in the forest, as it smells so sweetly of the trees,' replied Frieda, determined not to let Evadne's pessimism spoil her day. 'The way the sun shines through the branches, too, is very beautiful.'

'Oh, yes!' said Marie von Eschenau. 'It is like seeing patches of gold between the trees, when the sun shines. You will be surprised, Evadne; there are very few insects in the forest.'

They quietened presently, since the gradient was already beginning to increase slightly, and they knew that they would need all their breath for the hard work further on. All were keen and experienced climbers by now, and knew not to waste their energy unnecessarily; still, this climb was more strenuous than their usual expeditions.

At the edge of the forest, Miss Bettany announced the second tracking game.

'In the days of the pioneers in America, they would literally blaze the trail by cutting the bark of trees to expose the white wood, to show the way. Here, the Lieutenant and Matron have stuck split twigs into the bark: this doesn't hurt the trees as much, but the fresh breaks in the twigs show up a good long distance. Your task is to follow the signs through the trees, and to meet Lieutenant and Matron on the other side.'

Some of the girls looked a little dubious at the idea of crossing the forest simply by following signs on the trees, and Miss Bettany immediately reassured them. 'This time, you will all cross in a group. Joey, you'd better leave Rufus with me. No-one will get lost, and we shall make sure that you see the first signs in the trees as you go along, so that you can learn what they look like for yourselves. Are you ready?'

'Yes, Captain!'

'Then, who can see the first "blaze", and tell us which way to go?'

The girls stared intently at the pine trees. It was not easy to spot the 'blaze' without knowing what it should look like, and for a moment they were silent in concentration.

'Captain!' Mary Burnett called for her Headmistress's attention. 'I can see it on that tree there!' and she pointed to indicate the direction.

'Well done, Mary! That's the way to go. Keep your eyes peeled, girls, as the next one shouldn't be too far away.'

Gradually, the School made its way across the forest, the girls taking it in turns to look for the next blaze, and all managed to find them without too much difficulty. The mistresses at the rear of the party made sure to remove the signs, so that they would not confuse anyone else who should use the forest to lay a trail in the future.

Above the pine forest, and before the worst part of the climb, lay a grassy stretch, dotted with gentians, heartsease and cornflowers. Here they paused for a short rest, in order to 'gather their spirits', as Miss Bettany said, and share slabs of chocolate and coffee from their flasks. Rufus sat panting, as his huge fur coat made him much warmer than the girls: he was ready to be patient now, as he had enjoyed his long walk, and Joey made sure that he had a good drink of water before turning to her own coffee.

Before any girl was allowed to move on, she had to make sure that the area in which she had been sitting showed no sign of litter; no Guides worth the name, according to Baden-Powell, ever leave a camping ground dirty, and the same should apply to a picnic place.

Even such a short break left some members of the party disinclined to leave their pretty dell, but the mistresses would allow no straggling, and the girls had to move on together.

The sight of the valley down below made Joey want to sing aloud, and, before she was able to stop herself, she had broken into a favourite song, 'My Bonny Lass She Smileth'. But although Joey's voice was clear and pure, her song was short lived, as the toughest part of the walk required all her breath and concentration. It was a narrow, rocky path, bordered by limestone boulders, with very little greenery at all, and although it took only half an hour or so to traverse, it left the girls with no extra breath for 'frivolities', as Joey put it.

'I shall be glad,' remarked Gertrud Steinbrücke to her fellow-prefect Bernhilda Mensch, 'when we have reached the Sonnalpe and are able to have our lunch.'

'Yes, and the baskets will be much lighter then!' So saying, Bernhilda hefted one of the lemonade baskets from her right hand to her left. 'Did I not hear Madame say that we should picnic in the meadow behind Herr Doktor Russell's chalet?'

'Oh, Bernhilda, let me take that basket. You have carried it for quite long enough.' Gertrud paused to consider her reply. 'I believe that we are picnicking in the garden of the chalet, and we may also be able to see where the Sanatorium is to be built. Of course, we could not eat inside the chalet, as it is not much furnished yet.'

'It is not much furnished because he has not yet a wife,' Bernhilda remarked sagely.

They had at last reached the part of the Sonnalpe that led to the doctor's chalet, and Dr Russell was striding across the lawn to greet them, a wide grin upon his face.

'Welcome, one and all!' he announced, clasping Miss Bettany's hand. 'If you will follow me, I'll show you where to wash. By the right, quick march!'

Laughing, he led them across the small patch of grass in front of the building, and round to the pump and trough which provided the chalet with water until more modern plumbing was to be installed.

In the meadow behind the doctor's chalet, the school found Stéphanie and her cousin Aurélie waiting for them alongside Mr Denny's sister, who had brought a basket of delicious-looking honey-and-nut cakes with her. The two girls had been escorted up the mountain after Saturday's Guide meeting, so that they could spend time visiting Stéphanie's mother, who was increasingly frail as the weeks passed. Dr Russell was doing tremendous work for her, but she was very ill. Stéphanie's father was a naval man, and necessarily absent for long periods, so the girl and her mother were all in all to each other.

Joey was anxious to tell Miss Denny all about Guides, and she scarcely paused for breath as the words tumbled out.

'Of course, we're all working towards our Second Class tests, so that we can pass them, and some of us might get our Second Class this term if we try hard enough, and then we can do badge work. We're learning some Ambulance work this term, because it's so useful, and I'm aching to do Writer and Book Lover, and I want to do Swimmer too, if it's still warm enough when I've got my Second Class. But it doesn't leave much time for work,' she finished meditatively, aware that she was so full of enthusiasm for Guides that her school work was definitely taking second place. Miss Denny was, after all, a mistress, and thus could be expected to take a somewhat dim view of such a situation.

Jo considered a moment. They had already been warned that some of them would do better if they concentrated on school work during school hours. and that their marks across the term would affect their forms in the coming year. Joey suddenly realised that she herself could be counted among that number, and resolved to apply her brain a little more to her studies.

'Well, perhaps badges could wait until the winter, when we can't go out so much,' she concluded. She patted Rufus, and offered him some of her sandwich.

'Were you a Guide when you were younger, Miss Denny?' asked Simone, as she helped herself to a cake from the plate that Margia was proffering.

'No, no, I was too old to join in when the first company opened, but I very much liked to see the Guides who met in the next town. They often came round doing good works. I remember at harvest time, they always brought over baskets of delicious-looking food for the elderly people who lived next door to us: they couldn't get out easily on their own, so we would get oddments of shopping for them from time to time, and the Guides also liked to help.'

'*Quelle bonne idée!*' commented Simone. 'Perhaps we should do something like that for the poor people who live by the lake?'

'On top of the rest of the work we're doing?' Grizel too was beginning to feel the strain of the standards she had set herself at the beginning of the term.

'Well, we need not go to the lengths of growing fruit and

vegetables for the villagers quite yet; but they might like to receive some of the things that we make in Hobbies,' Rosalie suggested.

'Either that, or when we have our folk festival, we could have a collection at the end of that to "help the poor of the parish", as they say in churches,' Jo put in.

She had had the original idea of the folk entertainment at the end of their very first folk-dancing lesson, back at the beginning of the winter. Later on, towards the end of that term, the girls had begun to formulate ideas for a folk festival, inviting their parents and the hotel visitors to watch them dance the English country dances that they had learned and listen to the folk songs of their countries. By now, plans were well in hand, and everyone was hard at work practising.

'That sounds like a splendid idea,' interpolated Miss Denny. 'I know my brother has picked some madrigals for you to perform, along with the more traditional English folk songs. After all, "Greensleeves", as a madrigal, is just as "folk" as "Green Broom".'

'That was one of the ones that Bernie wanted us to sing,' meditated Jo. 'She said that she liked it very much. I remember, 'cos she got the name of the song wrong, and thought it was "Green Brooms". There's also those Appalachian Nursery Rhymes of mine.'

'Oh, Jo, must you start singing them again?' Grizel groaned. 'It was bad enough that you sang them pretty much without ceasing when Maynie first gave you the book!'

'Well, I wouldn't sing them non-stop any more, old thing!' laughed Jo. 'I really don't think I could bear the pained look on your face if I sang them in your vicinity again!'

'I wouldn't just *look* pained, I would feel pained! I was tired to death of all of them—no, *don't* start singing them again!' Mischievous Jo had taken a deep breath, and looked as though she were about to break into song. 'This may be a picnic, but it's still a meal, and not singing practice!'

Jo laughed.

'Poor old thing. I was only teasing. Here! Have one of these luscious cakes,' and she passed across the plate of honey-nut cakes. 'No, Rufus. They are not for you! Thanks awfully, Miss Denny! They were scrummy!'

'I'm glad you've enjoyed them, Jo.'

'Ouf, yes. And now all I want to do is lie in the sun and go to sleep!'

'Lazybones!' retorted Grizel. 'What you need now is a nice stroll round the garden!'

'Later, maybe. Why don't you go and ask Stéphanie? I think she'd like to do something more energetic!' and Jo pointed to the French girl, who, not having made the climb up the mountain, had not eaten nearly as much as the rest of the Chalet School's pupils, and was starting to look a little fidgety.

Grizel got up from her blanket, and wandered across the lawn to where Stéphanie was sitting.

'Would you like to come for a walk round the garden? Joey's so full of food, all the lazy little thing wants to do is sleep!'

'Thank you, yes. That would be pleasant. Perhaps you could explain to me the Union Jack again, as I am still not sure?'

'I'd be happy to,' replied Grizel, pleased to be asked. Her abrupt style often prevented the younger pupils from asking for her help, but Stéphanie had no such qualms, recognising that her Patrol Leader had a keen mind and liked to show off her knowledge. They wandered away, chatting quietly.

Rosalie Dene, meanwhile, was talking to some of the prefects about the idea of having a collection at the folk festival at the end of term.

'I think that is a very good idea, Rosalie,' replied Luigia di

Ferrara, the daughter of an Italian diplomat. 'Papa speaks often about those who have not our advantages, and how we should help them. We should have a collection for them,' she agreed.

'As Guides, we should have a bigger outlook, and this would encourage it,' said Juliet, mulling it over in her mind. 'Of course, we'd have to ask Madame's permission.'

'A vote! We should have a vote!' suggested Luigia. 'Gisela, may we have a vote, and, if everyone is agreed, ask Madame?'

'Yes, I think that would be the best way to proceed. I shall ask Madame if we may have a meeting before *Abendessen*, and then, if all are agreed, we shall ask her for permission to make a show again.' Gisela paused. 'I shall ask her now, so that I may tell the rest of the School before we go back down to the lake.'

She got up and walked over to where the Staff of the School sat, and, slightly haltingly, asked permission. This was readily granted, and she hurried back to her fellow-prefects with the news.

The School lay in the garden in attitudes of repose, sheltered from the heat of the day by their parasols. As Miss Bettany remarked, these weren't a particularly Guide-like article, but they were very useful on warm days. Far better to have a parasol than a batch of sunstroke cases in the School's san. At length, though, she decided that the girls had had enough rest, and they should start back down the alpe.

'On our way down, I would like you to collect flowers, leaves, stones, twigs and feathers—all manner of natural things—as we shall have a special Hobbies Club after *Abendessen* where you'll learn to make cardboard boxes and then use all the things you have collected to make pictures inside them.'

The girls were very much taken with this charming idea, and, accordingly, bent their minds to collecting an assortment of different leaves and flowers, and planning their pictures. Some of the more creative minds among the girls wondered if they might be able to manufacture some sort of room scene, or perhaps a dolls' house made of several different natural rooms, and they chattered happily on their way down the mountainside, and in the ferry across the lake as they made their plans, forgetting, for the while, about matters of Guiding.

Later that evening, before *Abendessen*, the whole school crammed itself into the Middles' formroom—with so many girls, it was something of a squash. The Seniors sat on chairs and window sills, while the Middles wedged themselves on to desks, and the Juniors sat on the floor. Joey had the Robin on her lap, while Margia was doing the same for her little sister, Amy. Small though the younger girls were, they were quite heavy enough, and Margia in particular was wondering whether her legs would go to sleep before the meeting was over.

'Quiet, please!' called Gisela, standing up next to the porcelain stove, and using her hand to steady herself when the Juniors sitting immediately in front of her jostled her legs as they made themselves comfortable. Fortunately the stove was unlit during the hot summer weather, otherwise she would probably have burnt her hand, a mishap that would have been frowned upon as being entirely avoidable. As silence fell, she continued.

'Thank you. Most of you know why we are here, and I do not want to keep you squashed in here for any longer than is necessary. Several of you have suggested that we should raise some money to help the poor people of the parish as part of our work as Guides. Naturally, we have to ask Madame's permission to do this, but before we do, I would like to know that you all agree with the idea. Please raise your hands if you would like to do this.'

To a girl, the School raised its hands to signify its agreement. There was no need to count the number of arms waving in the air, since it was obvious that they agreed by an overwhelming majority; some of Juniors had in fact raised both hands, having taken Gisela's instructions literally. She stood for a moment, smiling broadly, her eyes shining like stars.

'Quiet, please!' she cried, effectively dampening the murmur that had arisen as the girls realised that they were all of one mind. 'I can see that we all agree with this idea. I shall ask Madame for permission to hold our folk entertainment at the end of term in aid of the people of the lake, and I hope that I shall be able to tell you that she agrees.'

Gisela slipped out of the classroom and hurried to the Headmistress's study, knocking on the door. She paused to catch her breath, waiting for an invitation to enter the room. Once in front of Miss Bettany's desk, she quickly explained the reason for calling the meeting.

'So, you see, we have all voted to have a collection at the end of the folk festival, if we may, to help other people. We thought that it would be very fine and Guide-like to do this.'

'I agree—it's a simply splendid idea! And I like your suggestion that we should give any money we may collect after the folk festival to Vater Johann to distribute among the parish.' Miss Bettany paused. 'I shall come and talk to you all, as I would like everyone to hear what I have to say.'

She got up from her seat, and crossed the room with Gisela and they walked to the formroom.

There, Miss Bettany's low, musical voice carried clearly across the crowded room as she praised her pupils. 'As a Guide company, it is important that we raise money for those less fortunate than ourselves; perhaps during Hobbies you might like to consider making small gifts for some of the children in the area. I'm sure they'd appreciate a jigsaw puzzle, or a scrap book, or anything that will help them to pass the time in the winter.' Miss Bettany smiled at the eager faces looking up at her. 'I am proud to think that my girls are so generous and thoughtful, and willing to give up their time for such a worthy cause,' continued the Headmistress. 'You are all learning how to be true Guides, and showing that you understand that Guiding goes deeper than wearing a uniform and earning badges. Our Lord Himself said, "Inasmuch as ye have done it unto the least of these my brethren, ye have done it unto me." It is important to look after those less fortunate than ourselves, because to neglect them would be to neglect God Himself.'

The girls looked thoughtful, and many vowed inwardly to do their best to help other people, and to follow their Lord's instructions.

Chapter IX

'Adieu, Sweet Lovely Nancy'

The strains of Wilbye's 'Flora Gave Me Fairest Flowers' drew to an end, and the School's singing master looked satisfied. His health had improved enough to allow him to descend to the lake once a week in order to teach the Chalet School pupils. Tall and gaunt, with long brown hair cascading into his eyes and past his collar, he was a striking figure, and his mode of dress only served to augment this impression. His fondness for the romantic period led him to eschew a tie in favour of a bow, and his jacket was positively dandyish in cut. This was his first lesson with the girls for many weeks, and they were particularly anxious to please him.

'And now, maidens, we will move away from the Elizabethan period, and look towards something a little more recent. Your gracious Headmistress wishes you to learn some folk songs for the entertainment at the end of term, and I have selected two from England for you to try today. First, something which is new to you all, to freshen your minds.' He tossed his hair out of his eyes, and indicated to Cyrilla that she should collect up the song sheets. 'Margia, will you kindly distribute these? This is a song which was first recorded in writing at the end of the last century, but of course it is older than that.'

'Yes, Mr Denny.'

Margia collected the sheets from the music master and swiftly distributed them among her compeers. They looked excitedly at the printed music, which contained a setting of 'Adieu, Sweet

'ADIEU, SWEET LOVELY NANCY'

Lovely Nancy', a traditional English song, which tells the story of a sailor who is going to fight in the war overseas, and who promises to write to his sweetheart from all the foreign lands that he will visit while he's away:

> Adieu, sweet lovely Nancy, ten thousand times adieu,
> I'm a-going across the ocean, love, to seek for something new.
> Come change your ring with me, dear girl, come change your ring with me,
> For it might be a token of true love while I am on the sea.

The girls scanned the verses closely, keen to find out whether the sailor would come back to his sweetheart at the end of the song, and were a little surprised to find that, while he *was* going to come back home, he would go away again once all the money he had earned was spent.

> But when the wars are all over there'll be peace on every shore,
> We'll return to our wives and our families and the girls that we adore.
> We'll company court merrily, we will spend our money free,
> And when our money it is all gone we'll boldly go to sea.

Joey wondered to herself if Stéphanie's father was one such sailor, and then dismissed the thought. It did not seem as though the sailor in the song felt much remorse for his behaviour, and she did not believe that Stéphanie's father could so lightly leave his daughter behind when his work took him away from home.

Further speculation was swiftly curtailed, as, feeling that he had given the girls ample time to peruse the words and the music, Mr Denny coughed gently to attract their attention from the sheets.

'Mademoiselle, please would you be so kind as to give the keynote?' he asked in his usual courteous manner. 'Now, gentle maidens, will you sing the air?'

The girls did their best, and produced a reasonably creditable rendering of the tune. Margia the musical noted with interest that, in some phrases, the notes fell off the beat; she remembered 'Plato's' strictures against 'syncopated trash' in the first lesson he had given the girls, and was intrigued to realise that this folk music was not included in that category.

'This is, perhaps, a little harder than you are used to, is it not? Sit and listen: I shall tap the time and sing the song so that you may hear how it fits together.' Raising his voice in its sweet baritone, he sang the first verse to them. 'Now,' he asked, looking round at them with a piercing gaze, 'do you hear how it fits to the beat?' The girls nodded. 'Well then, let us try once more. Mademoiselle!'

The second attempt was much better, but nothing short of perfection would serve for 'Plato', and he wished them to have the tune and the rhythm firmly in their heads before they tackled the words.

'Pray, remain standing. This time, I would like you to march on the spot in time to my baton's taps, while I sing the song again. This will help you to fix the beat in your head. Then we shall try again, with all of us singing and marching.' This proved very much more successful, and presently they were ready to add the words, and soon they were singing the rollicking song with vim and vigour.

'That went very well,' said Mr Denny, nodding in satisfaction.

'Now, something a little simpler, as we lack the time for more difficult rhythms. Please, Frieda, collect the sheets, and Simone, distribute these.'

Quickly and efficiently, the old sheets were collected up and the new sheets distributed, on which were printed the ballad 'Brown Adam', one of many collected by Francis James Child at the end of the century:

> Oh who would wish for the wind to blow or the green leaves to fall therewith
> And who would wish for a far better love than Brown Adam the smith.

'Seems a bit soppy to me,' remarked Evadne as she read the first verse.

> But when he came to his lady's bower door and he stopped there a little way away
> There he spied a full false knight come a-tempting his lady gay.

Margia had made it a little further down the page. 'Oh no, it gets much more interesting,' she replied. 'There's a knight errant, who isn't a very nice knight.'

> 'Well I love Brown Adam well,' she says, 'and I know that he loves me
> And I would not give Brown Adam's love for any false knight that I see.'

> He's taken out a purse of gold that was full unto the brim
> 'Oh grant me love oh love lady, and this shall all be thine.'

'Well I love Brown Adam well,' she says, 'and I know that he loves me
And I would not give Brown Adam's love for all that you could give.'

Then he's taken out a long broadsword and he's flashed it all in her eye
'Oh grant me love oh love lady or through you this shall go.'

And sighing said this gay lady, 'Brown Adam he tarrys long,'
Then up there jumped him Brown Adam says, 'Lady I'm here at your hand.'

Well he's made him leave his bow, and he's made him leave his brand
And he's made him leave a far better thing—four fingers of his right hand.

'Coo, it's a bit bloodthirsty!' remarked Jo, as she scanned to the end. 'Seems a bit drastic to cut off the knight's fingers.'

'But it is very romantic,' replied Simone, 'that the lady should scorn the knight for her true love.'

'True. But I bet the money could come in handy,' said Jo, ever the pragmatist.

Their conversation was interrupted by Mr Denny tapping his baton on the music stand and demanding their attention. He frowned at the chatterers, knitting his dark brows, before once more asking Mademoiselle for the note.

'Fair maidens,' he said peremptorily, 'we shall see how quickly you can learn this song.'

'ADIEU, SWEET LOVELY NANCY'

Without the difficult rhythms of the previous song, and at a slower pace, the Middles found it easy enough to learn, and the singing master was unstinting in his praise of them at the end of the lesson.

'Well done, my maidens. You have proven today that music is, indeed, a gift of the gods to this earth. You have concentrated very well.'

Mademoiselle nodded in agreement: the pupils of the Chalet School were expected to give their full attention to their lessons, and generally did so.

'Dismissed. The elder maidens are at the door already, and await their turn!'

Clattering out of the hall, the Middles were obliged to hold their tongues until they reached their formroom: the rules at the Chalet School were few, but they were strictly adhered to, and the girls were mindful that any breach would bring retribution of one sort or another, either in the form of fines or lines to learn. Safely in the formroom, however, it was another matter, and they let themselves go, chattering like a tribe of magpies in a perfect Babel of languages.

'For folk songs,' remarked Margia, 'those were rather fun. Nothing like those Appalachian things of yours, Joey.'

'There was nothing wrong with those, you goop!' retorted Jo Bettany, bristling.

'They're mighty fine songs!' put in Evadne, keen to defend her native country's traditions; although her mother was Austrian, the youngster felt American to the core, and wished she could spend more time in that country. 'I'm going to sing one of them at the folk entertainment, you'll see.'

'Which?' Joey answered in a flash, before Margia had a chance to explain that she had not meant to criticise the Appalachian songs. Given the way her friends had reacted, she rather wished that she had not raised the subject at all.

'"Go and Tell Aunt Nancy"! That's rather fun, or perhaps "The Tottenham Toad". It does go on rather, though.'

'Oh yes! Perhaps Bernie could accompany you on her violin. They did, you know,' Joey responded, if a little incoherently. 'You know. Fiddling an' such.'

'I'll ask. I'll be gum-swizzled if I don't.' Evadne's vocabulary was still somewhat colourful, particularly when she felt strongly about something.

'Watch out! If a prefect hears you saying that, you'll get fined.'

'Why should a prefect hear me? They're all in Mr Denny's lesson!' Evadne's logic was perfect. 'They didn't notice Jo calling you a goop—they couldn't have!'

'Well, a mistress then. Honestly, Evadne. Sometimes I think you positively go searching for trouble.' Margia looked at her friend in exasperation. 'Anyhow, what did you think of today's songs?'

'Me, I liked them,' Aurélie remarked. 'Although I did not understand them, the melodies were pretty.'

'And so romantic!' sighed Simone. 'That the Lady should turn down the *richesse* of the Knight, to stay with her true love, Brown Adam. And the Sailor stay true to his Sweet Nancy.'

Simone had been one of the few girls in the School to think that 'Plato' himself was a romantic figure: the rest had followed Jo's lead in thinking that he looked, as Jo put it, 'rather an ass' with his bobbed hair and bohemian ways. Simone had enough sense to realise that her beloved friend would shy away from any romantic notions she might air, so she generally kept her opinion to herself in such matters.

'I did like the rhythms in "Sweet Nancy"—not like Plato at all: it was almost a kind of syncopation in some phrases, you know, and I thought he hated that. Perhaps he's loosening up with the summer sun!' giggled Margia.

The idea of 'Plato' unbending in the summer sun provoked Joey to snort with laughter. 'Just like his ideas for eurhythmics! Ooooh-ooooh! Can you imagine?' and she doubled over. Her mirth was catching, and soon the whole class was giggling.

'Still,' she continued, wiping her eyes as she gradually regained control of herself, 'd'you think that we could use those songs, as well as "Summer is Icumen in" and, oh, "Green Broom", for Folk Song and Dance badge? Not this term, but next term; my sister wouldn't let us try for it this term, as there's far too much going on.'

'Let us see,' replied Marie, going to her locker to hunt out her copy of *Girl Guide Badges*. 'Where is it—oh, at the end. That *is* odd. "Folk Song and Dance badge. This may be sewn on to the patrol flag of any patrol where at least four Guides have passed the following tests"—well, that explains why it is at the back; it is a group effort—"1. Be able to dance four Country Dances, if possible those peculiar—"'

'Peculiar dances? Well, some of them do have the strangest names!' interrupted Simone.

'"Those peculiar,"' she continued, glaring at her interlocutor, '"to their County or District. 2. Be able to sing (together) four Folk Songs, if possible those peculiar to their County or District."'

'And some of Plato's songs are so peculiar as to be downright weird,' Joey replied.

'You'd have to get Juliet's permish,' Margia put in, 'and I'd have to ask Gertrud. And poor Simone and Frieda. You'll never manage to persuade Grizel to do this one. She hates folk songs with a vengeance.'

'Don't I know it,' quoth Jo gloomily. 'Still, the rest of us could have a shot at it. We'll have done all the work by the end of term, and that'll be one more to get easily without too much strain.' She brightened a little. 'I bet Miss Durrant's already taught us the dances too. Where do we find out which ones we can do? Oh—it's the list produced by the same chap who collected my Appalachian Nursery Songs. Well, she's bound to have that—I'm sure I've seen it. Why don't we ask her over *Kaffee und Kuchen*?'

And so it was decided.

Chapter X

Escapades

IN the summer term lessons were often held outside, and outdoor activities generally were to the fore; Madame knew that when winter came they might face weeks on end of snowy weather when the girls could be confined to the house for several days at a time. That would give them ample opportunity to catch up on work they had missed in the course of the summer. During their playtime, too, the girls were chased out of doors at every opportunity.

Some of them, however, were unable to relax completely, as their heads were full of the Second Class tests, not to mention the badges they wished to try for later on. Several highly optimistic members of the school intended to try for three or four in addition to the Ambulance badge work which Miss Bettany had deemed a practical necessity, and they frequently found themselves with far too much to do, and not enough time in which to do it.

By now, though, it was their Guide work which tended to suffer rather than their lessons. The authorities had made it very clear that, should the girls produce bad school work, they would lose their Guide meetings, and, faced with such a threat, even the keenest Middles had settled down with a will.

The trouble was that the Second Class work was a lot harder than their Tenderfoot tasks had been, and many of the Guides were beginning to wonder if they hadn't tried to take on too much in one term. They were supposed to be working at their Hobbies, but all too often these had been set aside in favour of trying to make articles that were useful to the company and so passing one more part of the Second Class, thereby bringing the day when they could be tested for the other badges closer. After all, as Grizel had said, 'Our Motto *is* "Be Prepared", and I want to be as prepared as possible to be able to take some Guide badges as soon as I'm allowed to.' Her extremely forceful personality had led several of the more impressionable members of the community to fall in with her way of thinking before fully realising its implications, and the combined weight of their opinion had contrived to infect the rest of the school. She was a natural, if somewhat domineering, leader and always keen to rise to a challenge. It had been hard for her to find any teams against which to arrange match fixtures that term, and she found the idea of earning badges far more tempting, and, it must be said, vastly more rewarding.

Joey, at the centre of her own little coterie, was moodily darning a stocking. A year at the Chalet School with the influence of her Austrian friends, all of whom were excellent needlewomen, had improved her skill with a needle beyond all recognition. She would, however, never enjoy sewing, and was mending the stockings under duress. Finally completing the darn, she bit off the wool, and flung both stocking and needle into her sewing box.

'Oh, how I detest and *loathe* darning,' she sighed. 'It wouldn't be so bad, but the holes always come back again, and all that happens is that my stockings get more and more uncomfortable.'

Without bothering to look round, she stretched enthusiastically, swinging her arms like a windmill.

'Ow-w! Watch what you're doing, you goop! That was nearly my eye!' yelped Evadne, as she swung herself out of the way, almost knocking Marie von Eschenau off her chair in the process.

'Have you gone crackers, waving your hands about like that?'

In righting herself, Evadne had practically completed the process of dethroning Marie, who clung to the seat of her chair against further upset, sending triangles of black and yellow material cascading to the ground in the process.

'Evadne, please be careful! I shall fall off the seat if you do not pay more attention. Oh!'

'Sorry, Marie, I didn't realise you were quite so close to me. Joey was waving her arms around and nearly hit me. It's quite as much her fault as mine. Have you lost your needle or something?'

Marie, now steadier, had bent over at the waist, and with her chin on her knees was stretching forward and groping under the table.

'My thimble, actually,' she said in a muffled voice. 'It fell off the second time you knocked into me. Simone, will you help me to look for it, please?'

Simone was bristling at Evadne's opinion of Joey's behaviour, and was quite prepared to defend her friend to the hilt. An argument seemed to be brewing, and Marie, knowing how impatient Joey could be of Simone's championship, set aside her own ruffled feelings and tried to distract her.

With a reproachful glance towards the young American, Simone moved round the table towards Marie.

'Of course I shall help you. Do you think it may be under the table? Or that it could have rolled into a corner?'

'I'm not sure. We'd better try both,' and, so saying, Marie slipped from her chair and on to her hands and knees under the table. 'You go round clockwise on the outside and I'll go anti-clockwise on the inside,' she directed. 'Come on!'

Simone dropped obediently to her hands and knees, and proceeded to crawl in the opposite direction to Marie.

'I'm not crackers at all,' replied Joey calmly, after this brief hiatus. 'Anyhow, it beats sitting down and sewing! Marie, are those semaphore flags you're making?'

'Yes, but they are not yet tacked together properly. Be careful!'

Joey picked up the unfinished flags and began to signal, while Evadne watched, intrigued.

'Let someone else have a go, will you?' she cried, and she made a wild snatch for the flags.

'Show me you can read it first, and then I might!' returned Joey. 'Do you know semaphore?'

'No better than you knew Morse this week!'

At this, a general shout of laughter went up. At the previous Saturday's Guide meeting, Joey had mangled her attempts at Morse so much that her message came out in something closer to Dutch than English, and had made no sense in that either. Miss Maynard had been scathing over it, as she and Joey had spent enough time practising Morse Code in the holidays for her to feel the child should be fluent by now.

'There is no point in being in such a hurry to send your message that your dashes are no longer than your dots. You *must* make your dashes three times longer. Really, Jo, haven't you read the instructions in your handbook? Now go and think about the message, and write it down for me, *in Morse*, taking three times as long to draw the dashes as you do for making the dots. There is more to Morse than merely being able to recognise the SOS!'

Duly chastened, Joey had departed to write down the message. Her dashes were so long that she was only able to fit three letters to a line, and the message took up five sides of paper; she had taken Miss Maynard's instruction literally, counting laboriously as she wrote. Miss Maynard forbore to scold, however, as she recognised that the girl had done her best: and, although the phrase was hard to read, it was accurate.

'Go on! Let me have a go with the flags!' Evadne made another grab for one of the parti-coloured squares. 'Please?'

She reached for them again. Joey wasn't quick enough in moving them out of her way this time, and Evadne just caught a corner of a yellow triangle. She twitched it out of Joey's hand. Unfortunately, and as Marie had warned, the flags were not properly sewn; the yellow triangle came away with a nasty ripping sound, leaving Jo holding on to the black and standing very still as pins cascaded to the floor.

'Evadne!' wailed Jo, examining the frayed piece of cloth she still held. 'Now look! Oh, Marie. I'm so sorry. I'll sew it again for you!' And she sighed dramatically, before sitting back down at the table and reaching to pick up the pins.

'Gee, I'm sorry. I thought it'd hold up better than that. I'll pin it, and—' as Gisela announced bedtime for the Middles—'you can sew it tomorrow.'

'Better do the whole lot tomorrow,' replied Joey gloomily. 'No-one'll love us if we hang around pinning things together now. Oh, what a nuisance. I wish semaphore had never been invented!'

'You do not really mean that, Jo,' said Frieda, as they tidied up their work. 'It is such a useful way of communicating across distances when it is too far to shout, or even to yodel, and it may come in very useful one day.'

'Mm-mm,' answered Joey, distractedly considering the triangles of material, as she folded them up and put them away with the stocking in her work basket, before taking that to her space on the long shelf in the common room. 'Having to remake these flags will be a sickening nuisance!'

'Slang, Joey?' remarked Bernhilda, catching her words as she put away her own work basket, in preparation for leaving, as she and her sister Frieda slept at their parents' holiday home in Seespitz during the summer term. 'Put a fine in the box. You know Madame dislikes such ugly words. Please do not let me hear you use that one again!'

Grumbling to herself in an undertone, Joey complied with the Second Prefect's dictum, before wending her way to the Yellow dormitory. There her mood lightened somewhat, as she remembered that she had arranged to meet Marie and Simone outside the bathrooms so that they might all brush each other's hair simultaneously. It was forbidden to 'go visiting' between dormitories when they were supposed to be going to bed, but all had to clean their teeth and wash in the same room, which gave her the opportunity to say 'Goodnight' to her particular friends before separating for the night.

To have three quarters of the quartette sleeping in the same building was still something of a novelty. Simone had spent the previous two terms sleeping in Le Petit Chalet along with Frieda; but she had been moved back to the main chalet for the summer term as the space she had occupied in Le Petit Chalet was now required for younger girls. This change had inspired Jo to suggest the hair-brushing game, and they looked forward to including Frieda in the ritual next term when her parents would have left their summer home and returned to Innsbruck, and she would once again be a boarder.

Both Joey and Simone had short, dark bobs—Joey because her young life had been dogged by ill-health and her doctor had advised keeping her hair that way until she had outgrown that delicacy; while Simone, wishing to impress her idol, Jo, had cut hers in imitation during her first weeks at the Chalet School. Once the initial shock of her action had worn off, she had found that she was much cooler during the summer months without the heavy weight of hair. Her mother, as well as her cousin, Mademoiselle La Pâttre, had decided that it was best to keep it short while she was at school, and thus it had remained. Joey

Bettany, however, had been entirely unimpressed by this demonstration of affection, and had told Simone in no uncertain terms that she was an idiot, and that she cared neither whether her hair was cropped like a convict's, or as long as Lady Godiva's!

Marie's hair was a great contrast with that of her friends; her long, thick, golden locks required a great deal of brushing to remove all the tangles she acquired during the day, and her arms frequently began to ache before she had finished.

Joey finished cleaning her teeth first, and urged her friends to hurry up with theirs, brandishing all three hairbrushes in encouragement. Marie was the next to end her ablutions, and, eager to know how, exactly, this feat was to be performed, began to question Jo.

'How can we all brush each other's hair at once? If I'm brushing your hair and Simone's too, then how can you brush mine, when you will have your backs to me? And there wouldn't be room for your brushes on each other's heads either.'

'That's not how it works! I'll begin by brushing your hair, and then, when Simone's *finally* finished with her face, you can start brushing her hair and she can do mine. Then,' for Simone was starting to look distinctly disgruntled at the idea that Joey might brush someone else's hair and not brush hers, 'we'll all turn round, and I'll do Simone's hair, while you do mine, and she finishes off yours! It works like Empress Eugénie's Circle, like we did in Guides last week, but with hairbrushes instead of sitting down.'

'Oh, I see!' replied Marie, as Jo began brushing the heavy golden tresses. 'It is a shame that Frieda cannot be here to join us, as I am sure she would appreciate the help you are giving me.'

Marie was quite content to let her friend brush her hair, as she was very fond of Jo, though her way of showing it was very different from Simone's emotional fervour.

Simone rushed through the rest of her washing routine, and hurried across to begin brushing Jo's hair. They struggled a little with just the three of them, and had to call Evadne and Margia across to join them and make a circle rather than a triangle. The rhythmic strokes of Marie's brush down Simone's hair quickly soothed her ruffled feelings, and she was almost disappointed when she had to turn round and brush Marie's hair, while Joey brushed hers, as Jo's methods were brisk, to say the least of it. Meanwhile, Evadne's treatment of Marie's hair had been punctuated by occasional squawks from that lady as she tussled energetically with some of the tougher tangles. Having had much longer hair of her own in the past, however, Simone understood how to manage Marie's hair, and was quickly able to bring it under control.

All too soon it was time to part and go to bed; Marie was in Blue, and Simone was in Mauve with Margia, while Evadne and Jo were both together in Yellow. They returned each brush to its owner, and bade each other farewell for the night.

Lying in her bed, Jo was still awake when the Seniors came up. Despite the soothing ritual of brushing hair, Joey found her mind was still churning, trying to remember a mixture of semaphore signals, Morse Code and, for some reason, important dates during Napoleon's life.

She tossed and turned so violently that Juliet, the head of the dormitory, poked her head between the cubicle curtains to see what was wrong.

'I'm not surprised you're having difficulty sleeping,' she remarked in a low tone, taking in the rumpled state of the sheets and plumeau. 'Lie still, and I'll tuck you up again. I see you have some water already—do you need anything else?' she added, tucking Joey in with the same gentleness and skill that she had practised on the Robin. 'No? Well, be still and think peaceful thoughts. You'll soon drop off.' And, with a friendly pat, she left Joey and retired to her own bed.

Joey lay back and tried to do as Juliet suggested, vainly endeavouring to ignore the maelstrom of thoughts whirling round her head. Eventually she fell into an uneasy slumber, her dreams haunted by semaphore flags and huge dots and dashes, with sheet-bends and all the various hitches snaking round in a most unnerving manner. Although she was not, as a rule, given to nightmare, when she *was* troubled by bad dreams, the whole dormitory knew about it. Always a restless sleeper, tonight she tossed and turned even more energetically than usual, and once or twice she spoke (or, as Evadne would have put it, yowled) out loud.

At around one o'clock in the morning she began to flail wildly with her arms, throwing her rumpled covers back down the bed, and sat upright, muttering 'tivet, tikka, tikka' under her breath, imitating the noise of a 'dummy key'. She blinked, and was suddenly wide awake, as was her wont. As she pulled out her torch and checked the watch that she kept under her pillow, according to the usual practice of the denizens of the Chalet School, her face fell. It was far too early in the morning to be able even to consider reading, but she felt wide awake.

A thought occurred to her, and she swung her legs over the side of the bed and stood upright, before moving gently through her cubicle curtains and into the dormitory. It was a warm night, and it did not occur to her that it would be prudent to put on slippers and dressing gown. The Morse still ran through her brain, befuddling her slightly. 'Tivet, tikka, tivet,' she muttered, heading purposefully towards the door of the room. She opened it and passed through, moving towards the stairs. 'Tikka. Tikka, tivet.' If she was quiet enough, perhaps she could just creep downstairs and double check the infuriating dots and dashes in the book that was in her locker. If she just *knew* for sure exactly which way round the dots and dashes for 'F' and 'L' went, she felt that she would be able to get back to sleep again—and if she did not sleep, it would be hard to conceal that fact, as Jo had the type of colouring that lends itself to deep shadows under the eyes. Her sister would notice, and quite probably ask some awfully awkward questions about why she had not slept, and it would be difficult to explain that it was a case of confused Morse.

The click of the door as it shut caused Juliet, who slept nearest it, to awaken. She blinked a few times, before reaching under her pillow in her turn to check her watch. Seeing the hour, she yawned, and debated whether it was worth getting up to find out what exactly had woken her. Deciding that there would be no harm in checking the dormitory in case a window was swinging in the breeze, which might wake up the rest of the girls, she put on her dressing gown and slippers and picked up her torch. A quick glance at the windows revealed that they were tightly wedged in place with the window stops, and she decided to return to her bed. Something prompted her to check on the other girls for whom she was responsible, and she peered between the cubicle curtains on the way back to her own cubicle. Gertrud, Vanna, Paula and Rosalie were all sleeping peacefully, and did not stir as she shone her torch at the foot of their beds; the humps thus revealed told her that they were safely tucked in, while ensuring she ran no risk of waking them by an incautious flash of light on their faces.

Coming to Joey's cubicle, however, she realised that something was wrong. The curtains were not tightly closed, as they had been when she had tucked Joey in, and it was immediately obvious that Joey was not in bed, and, more worryingly, had not put on her dressing gown. Remembering how ill Joey had been when the first snows had fallen the previous winter, and that just from standing at the door, Juliet began to feel bothered. It was impossible to be too careful where Jo was concerned—this much had been dinned into the girls.

Drawing her fine, dark brows together, she frowned in concentration. There was no need for Joey to have gone looking for water, since her glass was still full. Juliet moved over to the bed, and felt the bottom sheet. It was still slightly warm, and she realised that the sound which had woken her had probably been the result of Joey's departure from the dormitory.

'Perhaps she felt ill, and went to see Matron,' she thought. 'In which case, I'd better check that she's safely there, and then go back to bed. It'll be easy to see if she is in the san, 'cos the light will shine out from under the door.'

She picked up Jo's yellow dressing gown, and prepared for departure. Knotting her own gown more tightly, and stuffing her torch in the pocket, she opened the door as quietly as she could, and shut it equally silently, by dint of pushing against it with one hand as she pulled it slowly closed with the other. Switching her torch back on, since it was a moonless night, she padded along the corridor towards Matron's room.

As she reached it, a sudden crash from one of the downstairs formrooms made her jump violently. She landed against Matron's door with a thump, and almost immediately a thin chink of light appeared. Although Joey had not, apparently, gone to wake Matron earlier, that redoubtable lady was certainly awake now. The door flew open and there she was, pulling on her red dressing gown over her nightdress, a look of concern on her face.

'Are you ill? What's the matter, lassie?' she asked, placing a cool palm on Juliet's forehead, her native accents more evident than usual as she too reluctantly left sleep behind.

'I'm not ill, Matron, but Joey isn't in her bed, and I thought that she might have come to find you if she was unwell. I'm sorry for waking you. There was a crashing sound downstairs,

137

which made me jump. D'you think it's burglars? What if they've taken Joey?'

'Burglars? Och, no dear, I'm sure it's not burrrglars!' with a tremendous rolling of the 'r', which would have left Juliet hard pressed not to giggle at any other time. 'Why, I saw Miss Bettany herself lock the doors this evening, and all the windows downstairs are tightly shut. But Joey's not in her bed, you say?'

Matron frowned. She most certainly did not like the idea of any pupil wandering around the Chalet in the middle of the night, and particularly not a pupil who was prone to illness.

A second door on the landing opened, revealing Wanda von Eschenau, her golden curls tamed into a waist-length plait. Looking in both directions along the corridor, she espied Juliet and Matron, and, closing the door behind her with an admonition to Marie, with whom she shared the Blue dormitory, to go back to sleep, she hurried along the corridor to join them.

'What was that noise? Do you suppose we have a burglar?' she inquired anxiously.

'A burglar, no. Joey Bettany, possibly,' replied Matron, frowning. She could see that the whole Chalet would soon rouse, convinced that the School was under some sort of siege, and would very probably be out of sorts the next morning as a result. Her instinct told her that she should get the girls back to bed as soon as possible, but she was torn by her concern for Jo. At that moment, however, the fitful light of a torch caught their attention as Miss Bettany hove into view up the stairs, closely followed by Miss Maynard, who looked distinctly worried.

'You and Juliet awake as well?' she asked Wanda. 'I've just sent Gisela and Grizel back to bed! It seems that the entire school's awake. Go back to your dormitories, please. Once I have found out the cause of that crashing noise, I shall go and make hot milk, and— What on *earth* was *that*?' as another crash occurred.

'Matron, Miss Maynard, I think we should go and investigate!' Miss Bettany looked decidedly agitated.

Matron took Jo's proffered dressing gown from Juliet, and the trio moved purposefully towards the source of the noises. Juliet and Wanda, meanwhile, returned to their respective dormitories, to settle their comrades who had been rudely awoken by what turned out to be Joey's latest effort.

Proceeding towards the classrooms, the three mistresses maintained a grim, determined silence. Although Matron suspected that Joey was the source of the noises, neither the Headmistress nor the Senior Mistress yet had any inkling that she might be involved. Neither knew that she was missing from her bed, and it is unlikely that either would have found this extra knowledge reassuring.

The door of the Middles' classroom was open, with light blazing through. They peered round the edge of the door and gasped. Standing in the middle of the floor, consulting her Guide handbook, her hair standing on end and her pyjamas rumpled, Joey presented an incongruous sight. Despite the care she had taken to move quietly, she had fallen over the waste paper basket—left by some careless person in the middle of the floor—on the way to her locker; and on her way back towards the light switch, rubbing her knee as she went, she had tripped once again, sending a folding desk flying as she stumbled. She looked up, startled, and was horrified to see the three members of staff.

'Josephine Mary Bettany, what on *earth* are you doing?' Miss Bettany was the first to recover from the shock of seeing her errant sister in a completely unexpected place.

Joey stared at her.

'I couldn't sleep for thinking about Morse, and in the end I *had* to get up and check it. I was right about what I was wrong about, too!' she answered confusedly. 'I think I'll be able to sleep now that it feels straighter. I'm very sorry. I didn't think.'

'Give me the book at once. You will go with Matron who will put you straight to bed, yes, with hot milk, and there you will stay until it appears you have regained your senses. No, I do not wish to hear another word from you. You have been extremely naughty, and have shown a complete disregard for whatever common sense you may possess. Yes, I know you've apologised, but that doesn't alter the fact that you have managed to wake most of the Chalet with the noise you made!'

Miss Bettany was extremely angry with her younger sister, and Joey wilted under her glare. Crestfallen, she took her dressing gown from Matron, put it on, and, wearing a hangdog expression, preceded her up the stairs to the san.

Later on, as Joey settled down to sleep, having swallowed a mug of warm milk under Matron's watchful eye, the staff discussed the situation in undertones. They had seen to it that every girl who was awake had been provided with hot milk, and the Chalet was peaceful once again.

'Och, to be honest, I think she's just been trying to do too much. What with school work, exam work and Guides as well, they've all been doing a great deal; and in this heat, it really isn't a guid idea. I'll let her sleep as long as she will in the morning. Would you let the school as a whole have an extra half-hour to make up for tonight's interruptions?'

As chief keeper of the school's health, Matron had powers that not even the Headmistress would gainsay.

'Yes.' Miss Bettany roused herself from her reverie. Joey's health had been a continual worry to her from early childhood onwards. Although she had not actually been sleepwalking, Jo had never before been so agitated that she had got up during the night, and this new development was alarming. Madge resolved to telephone Dr Russell at the Sonnalpe in the morning and ask his advice. She worried that, despite the warm night, Jo could have caught cold, or be starting something more serious.

'You're right. All the same, don't you think it would be a good idea to have Jem down, or perhaps Dr Erckhardt?' she asked. 'Just to make sure it's nothing serious? She must have been thoroughly overstrung; she's never been in such a state that she's got up in the middle of the night before. I don't think that it's possible to be too careful where Jo is concerned.'

Miss Maynard and Matron exchanged glances.

'I think, my dear, that would be a very good idea. Now perhaps we could brew some coffee; you look as though you could do with it!' replied Miss Maynard.

Miss Bettany nodded, and together they headed down to the kitchen, while Matron made sure that her patient was firmly tucked in. She was determined not to have any further escapades that night.

Chapter XI

AN EDICT

'WELL, old lady, you've given us all quite enough trouble!' Thus Dr Russell, putting his stethoscope away. 'I think that the best place for you, for the next day at least, is bed. That way we'll know exactly where you are!'

'But I'm not *ill*!' retorted Joey, apparently none the worse for her unwonted outing the previous night. 'I feel fine! Why should I have to stay in *bed*—' injecting the word with such a tone of disgust that it had to be heard to be believed—'all day? Can't I at least sit up on the settee in Madge's study?'

'Sorry, old thing, can't be done. The best thing for you is to sit tight and quiet for a bit. Tomorrow I *might*—and I mean "might", so don't get too optimistic—let you get up. That's assuming that you don't go toddling round the school at an unwarrantable hour, making a complete and utter nuisance of yourself again tonight.'

He turned and smiled at Madge. 'I'll leave a tonic for her as well. Make sure she takes it three times a day for the next week. She may go back to morning lessons tomorrow *if* she's well enough, but unless it's one of Mr Denny's days or perhaps an art lesson, keep her out of afternoon lessons for a couple of days longer. She is overwrought and needs a proper rest.'

He pulled a bottle out of his case and handed it over, before gathering together his belongings in preparation for departure.

'Thank you for coming down,' said Madge, as they left the

patient to Matron's care. 'She really did give me a shock, besides disturbing the entire school.'

'Well, she's a growing girl, and I think that she's been overdoing it rather. She is easily excited, and she's just chosen a more dramatic method than usual of expressing herself. A day in bed, with complete rest from *any* type of work, should sort her out. And that,' he remarked with a chuckle, 'includes trying to write another Elsie book.' The previous term had seen Joey laid up with a badly sprained ankle, and she had amused herself by writing a sizeable tract entitled *Elsie's Boys*. 'Don't let anyone visit her—in fact, she's probably best left to herself as much as possible. The important thing is to make sure that she doesn't think she's done anything particularly clever by meandering around in the middle of the night, no matter how hard she is finding it to go to sleep.'

'And keeping her in bed, which she absolutely loathes, will do that. She sees bed as more of a punishment than anything else.'

'Precisely. If she likes, she may read something, but nothing too stimulating. Sewing or embroidery would probably be a better occupation, though. I can't think that sock darning could be anything but soothing.' Indeed, Jem's mother had been the most placid of creatures, rarely seen without sock in hand, darning assiduously.

Madge laughed, and laid her hand on his arm as they walked out of the front door.

'Oh, Jem! Darning is *not* Joey's strong point, and, after the rumpus that occurred last week, when she was late for Guides after Matron kept her behind to finish the stocking that she's been mending for the past fortnight, I don't think she'd find darning very soothing at all.'

'Perhaps darning isn't the answer, then. I'm sure you'll think of something, my dear.' He kissed her gently on the cheek, and departed, raising his hat as he passed through the gate and out of the school grounds.

Madge waved at him as he walked off, and returned to her pupils. She was taking the Seniors for English Literature, and although she had been prevented from giving her planned lecture by Joey's visit from Dr Russell, they had not been idle in her absence, and were engaged in reading aloud the first act of *As You Like It*. She waited until they had finished their scene before applauding their efforts.

'Well done, girls! That was as good as some of the readings we used to have at my High School in Taverton. Your English has improved enormously over the past year.'

The Seniors exchanged pleased glances. The Chalet School was cosmopolitan in make-up, but all the girls cherished an ambition to be as 'English' as possible in all facets of their scholastic life. Miss Bettany's praise therefore pleased them greatly, especially as many of them would be leaving at the end of the summer term.

'Madame, how is Joey?' asked Juliet, her brow slightly creased with worry. She had had a strenuous night, and the shadows under her eyes were obvious, despite the extra half-hour's sleep allowed that morning.

'Very cross at having to stay in bed all day, but otherwise quite well. She seems to have suffered less from her escapade than the rest of us did,' replied Miss Bettany, knowing that the girls were anxious about their friend. 'We're going to keep her very quiet today, and we are sure that she will not repeat her behaviour. I know I can rely on you not to discuss this episode; and please make sure that none of the younger ones do either. The faster we all forget about it, the better.'

The girls knew by now that when Madame asked them not to

talk about a subject, it was best for all concerned to fall in with her wishes. Once something was forbidden it remained so, and they were on their honour to obey her even when left unsupervised. Most of the Seniors were prefects, and as such represented Miss Bettany's authority within the school. They therefore didn't hesitate to quash any Middle whom they found chattering away about Joey's latest exploit.

'But, it is only because I worry about her that I ask!' mourned Simone that lunchtime, having been roundly rebuked by Juliet after she heard the French child speculating about what might have caused Joey to go wandering round the school during the night.

'And you know full well that Madame does not want you to mention the matter among yourselves! If you had any questions, you should have gone to Madame, or Miss Maynard, or Matron, or any of the other members of staff, rather than asking Frieda, who you should have known would have no better idea about what was wrong than you do, particularly since she was at home! Oh, Simone, *when* are you going to learn not to cry at the least little thing?' For Simone had burst into tears. An immensely sensitive child, she really loathed being castigated in public.

Mademoiselle, coming upon the scene, immediately decided that Simone too was overwrought and promptly ordered her off to bed for the rest of the afternoon, whereupon Simone decided that she was being punished entirely unjustly and howled even more loudly. She had so far that term successfully checked her tendency to tears, and to find herself in disgrace when she first failed was even more upsetting. Mademoiselle hurried her cousin up the stairs to the pretty Mauve dormitory that she shared with Bianca, Margia and Suzanne Mercier, and helped her to bed.

'*Simone, tu vas te faire mal à la tête! Ne pleure plus!*'

admonished her cousin as she tucked the child into bed. '*Attends! Je te donnerai une tisane.*'

Mademoiselle departed to the kitchen to find Marie and procure the necessary ingredients. Simone, still gently weeping, rolled over and turned her face to the wall, her handkerchief clutched in her hand.

Mademoiselle was some time making the tisane, and by the time she returned to the dormitory, she discovered that Simone had dropped off to sleep. Gently, she wiped away the tears that still rested on the child's cheeks, and left her to rest.

Simone slept for almost an hour, and on waking felt much better for her nap. She told herself that, bad though bed was in the middle of the day, it could have been much worse. Mademoiselle's tisanes were notorious for their noxious scent and revolting taste, and she was relieved that she had missed that particular ordeal.

Kaffee und Kuchen saw Madge visiting her younger sister. Joey was thoroughly fed up by now, and had started tapping out Morse Code on her knees, muttering the sounds of the dummy key again. Madge's sharp ears caught the muffled noises before she entered the room, and she opened the door extremely quietly. Joey didn't notice her sister, so intent was her concentration.

'Tikka, tivet, tivet, tivet. Tikka, tikka, tikka. Tivet, tikka, tivet. Tivet. Tikka—'

'Tivet, tivet,' finished Madge. 'Bored, are you?'

Joey's face was a picture of horror. She was sure that practising Morse Code was most emphatically not what Jem had had in mind for her when he had condemned her to bed for the day, with such strict instructions to rest. She blushed hotly, and looked sheepish.

'Tell me, Joey,' said Madge, sitting on the edge of the bed in complete disregard of her own rules on the subject. 'Why are you practising Morse Code now? You've plenty of jigsaws to choose from, as well as a couple of books. And you can't tell me that you've read all the books in the library since we brought so many new ones back with us from England!'

'I don't want to get behind,' mumbled Joey. 'You see, Madge, I *do* so want to get my Second Class badge this term, and then I can start on some of the Guide badges. And I can't do that until I've got my Second Class badge, and if I sit here doing nothing I'll get behind …' She trailed off, aware that her sentences had 'gone round in circles' and that she was repeating herself.

'Get behind? Whatever do you mean?' queried Madge. She was not at all prepared for this sort of statement from Joey, who was usually the most happy-go-lucky of scholars, and who had never before worried about her position in form when she had been kept away from her classmates as a result of one of her frequent illnesses. Joey sat silent and made a vague gesture. 'You know that when you're ill we don't worry so much about how your school work is going. It's *far* more important that you get well and healthy again quickly, without worrying yourself ill again. What has made you worry about getting behind with things now?'

'It's not school work, Madge, it's Guides I don't want to get behind with! If I don't keep going with Morse, and knots, and Ambulance and so on, I'll never be ready for any tests!' The relief of telling her sister this caused Joey to burst into tears in an entirely uncharacteristic manner. She brushed them away hastily with the back of her hand, and looked at Madge.

Jo was in a sorry state. Her hair was all at sixes and sevens, her face blotchy from her unaccustomed outburst, and her dark eyes full of tragedy. Although the Bettanys were not a demonstrative family as a rule, Madge drew her younger sister into a brief hug.

'You silly thing!' she said affectionately, ruffling the golliwog mop still further. 'You've been trying to do far too much, and fit far more in than you're really able to, haven't you?'

Joey nodded, and made a muffled noise in reply.

Assuming that she'd said 'yes', Madge continued, 'I don't think you're the only one, either. Mademoiselle has just told me that she's sent Simone to bed in a thoroughly wrung-out state, and you're still none of you *really* giving of your best during lessons.' She put Joey away from her, and that young lady shook her head sadly. 'You've all become extremely keen on Guiding to the detriment of many of your other pursuits. All your hobbies seem to have turned to Guide work; I can tell that you haven't been making as many jigsaws as you did last term because you don't keep asking me for new blades for the saw. I think that you're trying to do more than you need to. Am I right, Joey-baba?'

Joey could tell that Madge wasn't really angry with her, just concerned for how she was. Knowing how much her sister worried when she was ill, she decided to come completely clean.

'It's not just Second Class we've been trying to learn. Er—er—someone said that it was a good idea to prepare for some of the Guide badges too, at the same time, so that we could take them quickly, and really have something to show for what we've done this term.'

The schoolgirl code of honour forbade her to mention the name of the culprit, but Madge quickly guessed who it might have been. She knew full well that of all her pupils, Grizel Cochrane was the keenest Guide in the school.

'And this is why you've all been working so madly! No wonder you've made yourself ill. Joey,' she continued more seriously, 'I want you to promise me that you won't try to do any more Morse Code until the end of the week. Or any semaphore with the Robin either. I shall help her if she wants to practise, so you needn't worry that you're letting her down.'

Joey smiled gratefully, as a weight lifted from her shoulders. She was reluctant to admit it, as she dearly loved the Robin, but the child's request for help with semaphore had proved trying to satisfy.

'Thanks, old thing!' she replied. 'I promise. As long as you're sure you'll have time to help the Robin?'

'I'll have time; I may be busy, but I'm not so busy that I can't do that for her. I think, however, that, since we're growing so much, I'll have to get another mistress for next term. But that's beside the point. I'm more worried about you and the amount of work you've been trying to do.'

'But it's so hard *not* to try and do Guide badge work! It *is* interesting, you know, Madge,' Joey replied anxiously. She was truly torn between wanting to do the work and needing some respite from it. 'As well as being good fun, some of it.'

'That's as may be. However, I'm going to issue an embargo on all Guide work that is not related to the Second Class badge. No-one will be allowed to work towards any extra Guide badges until after the summer holidays. Futhermore, the only time you should be thinking about Guide tests is on Saturdays, during Guides or during your free time on Saturday afternoon. You all have enough to amuse yourselves, without stewing indoors over badge work. That way you'll be able to concentrate properly, and do everything well. After all, a thing half done is a thing not done at all.' Madge smiled to herself, as she saw the palpable relief in Joey's face. This, more than anything, told her she had made the right decision.

As might be expected, the issuing of such an edict caused more than a few grumbles amongst some of the keener Guides in the school. The Cornflower patrol in particular felt the restriction bitterly. Grizel, as Patrol Leader, seriously considered asking that those who had only one more clause to fulfil before gaining the coveted Second Class award might be allowed to try for one Guide badge of their own choice, as there were still several weeks to go before the end of term. Her Second, Luigia, tried to dissuade her, even though she too was tempted by the idea; neither could see that Grizel's fanatical enthusiasm for Guiding had rubbed off on the rest of the pupils, and that it was because this had been carried to extremes that Miss Bettany had put her foot down.

'If Madame has so ordained, then we should obey. We have plenty of other things to occupy us before the end of term; as well as exams, we have the folk festival, and Madame's birthday too. We are not leaving at the end of this term, but Gisela, and Bernhilda, and Wanda are. If they are not complaining, how can we?' Luigia asked reasonably.

'But it's not as if we could camp, either, to take the edge off it!' cried Grizel, refusing to see that Miss Bettany's dictum was either just or sensible.

'That is true,' replied Luigia consideringly. 'But until Madame has her licence, we should not complain about not being able to camp, because we cannot do anything about it. We do not have any tents either, and I should not like to sleep outside without some sort of covering.'

'That's not the point, and you know it!' retorted Grizel feelingly. They were seated under the shadiest tree they could find, resting after the week's Guide meeting. It had been far too hot to do anything strenuous, and an hour's work at knots had tried even Frieda's patience to the point where she had become snappy and irritable, displaying signs of a temper that no-one had thought she had. 'Just because Joey was *stupid* enough to make herself ill by trying to do too much, we all have to suffer. If she weren't Miss Bettany's sister, nothing like this sort of fuss would have been made, but we all have to kowtow and meekly obey because Madame's little sister has been ill, and it was her own silly fault.' Grizel paused, her cheeks flaming. '*And* we haven't had any decent matches either, apart from those biddies in one of the hotels. I wrote and asked the new people at the Sonnalpe, and they won't come down, they're too busy, and I'm sure we won't be allowed to go up to them, because it'll be "too exhausting" to hike up there and then play cricket, or some such footling nonsense, and honestly, what's the *point* of it all?'

She flung herself flat on her back, and stared moodily up at the branches of the tree, the sunlight dappling her face. Luigia had no answer to this diatribe, and judged it wiser to hold her tongue for the time being. Instead, she buried herself in her copy of *The Jungle Book*, and was soon lost in the adventures of Mowgli.

Grizel, however, continued to stew silently. Starved of love at home, unable to win the approval of her stepmother, she felt, erroneously, that winning her Second Class badge and at least one Guide badge in the same term as she had been enrolled might at least give her parents something to boast about. Her sporting prowess was frowned upon, and she knew they were against her ambition to become a PT mistress when she left school; so much time, effort and money had been poured into making her a fine pianist that there was no hope that she would be allowed to do the one thing for which she not only had an aptitude, but which she also actively enjoyed. Grizel had been told by her piano master, Herr Anserl, that she had both the fingers and the soul of a machine. She was an extremely competent pianist, but her music lacked expression. As a Guide, Grizel was exceedingly smart and proud of herself, and she knew that, even if her stepmother disapproved of her achievements as a Guide, which seemed very likely, her father was still interested. He had, after all, bought her both the Girl Guide handbooks and several story books on the subject the term before the Chalet School had started its own Guide company.

While she mulled this over, Stéphanie Pagnol, who had at last completed nearly all her Tenderfoot tests, came over to her Patrol Leader to ask for some help with knots. Grizel sighed deeply since she was very bored with knots at that point, but, cognisant of her duties as Patrol Leader of the Cornflowers, creditably did her best to help the last member of her patrol overcome her difficulties with the sheepshank and the sheet-bend, while trying to help her remember which was which.

This kept her occupied until the bell rang to signal *Kaffee und Kuchen*, and Stéphanie's evident gratitude helped her to realise that there was more to being a Guide than simply winning badges and having fun camping. Grizel did not forget how the French girl's simple request and evident desire to do her best within her capabilities had soothed her where Luigia's logic had failed, and a friendship began between the two girls that was to prove beneficial to both.

Chapter XII

A Spot of Morris

CHATTERING, the Seniors made their way to the hall for their folk dancing practice with Miss Durrant. Folk dancing was more usually an exercise that occupied the winter months, when the girls were often confined to the chalet for days on end, owing to the fierce winter storms that raged in the Tyrol. More energetic than any other type of dancing, it provided the best exercise for growing girls, and the pupils of the Chalet School had embraced the pursuit wholeheartedly since the arrival of Miss Durrant two terms previously. They had learnt twenty dances over the previous winter, including such favourites as 'We Won't Go Home till Morning' and 'If All the World were Paper', which was particularly popular for its sung chorus. They had also, during the second term, begun to learn some morris, inspired by Miss Durrant's performance of the jig 'Jockie to the Fair' during one of their dancing sessions. So far, they had learnt how to 'step' correctly, and had mastered a dance using handkerchiefs. This was 'Laudnum Bunches', in the same tradition as 'Jockie to the Fair'—morris dances are grouped according to tradition, the tradition being named for the village where the dance originated.

The girls assembled in the hall, and Miss Durrant bade them stand in a circle.

'We will start with some stepping practice. Remember, you aren't being asked to bend your knees and pick your feet up alternately: what you must do is keep the knees straight and bring each foot *forward* alternately in a sharp swing! Mademoiselle! A one, and a two, and a three and a four! One-two-three-hop! One-two-three-hop!'

As the girls fell into the beat, she stopped counting and watched critically for a few bars, and gave pointers as she herself 'stepped' in time to the music.

'Very good, Grizel! Remember, swing the leg from the hip joint. Stéphanie, loosen a little! Better to have a slight bend in the swinging leg than to be so stiff! Bernhilda, if you don't swing your leg so far forward, you won't keep losing your balance. That's much better! Well done! Stay on the balls of your feet, girls! Your heels shouldn't touch the ground. And *don't* point your toes, as that is not folk, and particularly not morris!'

The girls were soon pink and breathless, and Miss Durrant let them rest for a moment before pairing them up to dance 'Laudnum Bunches', a corner dance for three pairs; the girls would have to take it in turns to sit out, as there was one over when they had made up two sets. Standing in columns, with their hankies held at their sides, the first set, made up of Gisela, Bernhilda, Bette, Vanna, Lisa and Wanda, looked as smart as any side dancing on the village green, for all that they weren't wearing traditional costumes. In turn, each set of corner couples came in to meet, passed by right, exchanged stations, turned a half turn clockwise to land in their opposite's place, and then repeated the sequence to land back in their original position: this was the 'chorus' of the dance. Then the whole set would dance a 'verse', before repeating the chorus.

The constant to-and-fro was entrancing to watch, and the hankies embellished the movements of the girls as they danced lightly—morris dancing, it must be remarked, is a mostly male tradition, and only some of its dances are suitable for women. The second set, consisting of Grizel, Gertrud, Rosalie, Mary, Juliet and Luigia took their turn and then, finally, Stéphanie was able to dance, along with the girls Miss Durrant felt would benefit from a second attempt.

'Remember, girls, teamwork here is just as important as teamwork on the hockey field, or in your patrols at Guides. You are not six individual dancers, but one team made up of six members. Look at each other, and pay attention to how your team mates are dancing. We're aiming for a unified approach!'

The girls threw themselves into the dance with renewed energy, and the improvement was palpable.

'Well done!' Miss Durrant announced at the end. 'That was definitely better than the first time round! You're nearly ready to show that dance at the festival. You've worked hard. Would you like to learn a new dance, now, with sticks instead of hankies?'

'Oh, yes please, Miss Durrant!'

'Good. Now, fold your hankies and put them over there, and take a stick each from the pile.'

She indicated a heap of sticks next to Mademoiselle's piano. Each was around seventeen inches long, and thick as a stout broom handle—indeed, they had been cut by Eigen, who usually helped with the heavy work in the kitchen, from a batch of broom handles brought up from Innsbruck the previous week. They were quite plain; although the morris men in Oxfordshire generally paint their sticks in bright colours for performances, these sticks were for practising, and there was no sense in painting them, as the paint soon flakes off with use.

'We are going to learn a dance called "Bean Setting"—the verses are just the same as in "Laudnum Bunches", but the chorus is entirely different. As, of course, is the tune. Mademoiselle, if you would be so kind?'

Mademoiselle struck into the new tune, and the girls bobbed in time to the music, feeling the difference between holding on to a stick in one hand, instead of hankies in both.

'Hold your stick towards the middle, and, when you are not using it, hold it vertically by your side. Don't let it stick out, or you run the risk of hurting someone! Now, the first thing we'll do is practise "dibbing".'

There were a few giggles among the girls at this: notwithstanding their age, they found it an extremely funny word.

'Dibbing, like in the garden?' asked Rosalie, whose father was a keen gardener in his spare time. 'When you use a dibber to plant seeds?'

'That's precisely it. The name of the dance gives a clue, doesn't it? So, face your partner, stoop over, and tap the end of your stick on the ground. And that's a dib. We do that on the first and second beat of the bar, and on the first beat of the next bar, still bending over, we hit sticks together. And then repeat for another two bars. The rhythm is "dib, dib, strike, rest".'

The girls bent over, and, after a few false starts, managed to beat their sticks on the floor in perfect time, and then clash sticks across the set.

'Well done. This is the first half of the chorus, and it's called "dib and strike". The second half of the chorus, we take it in turns to pass the "strike" round the set and then all strike across the set again. Go round the set anti-clockwise, and let's see how we do.'

The first few strikes worked beautifully, but as Stéphanie turned to strike Grizel's stick, she mis-aimed and caught Grizel's hand instead.

'Owwwwww!' Grizel dropped her stick and instinctively put her injured finger in her mouth, the better to soothe her hurt. 'That's nothing like being hit at hockey, but it still smarts a bit,' she remarked indistinctly.

'I am sorry, Grizel. I did not mean to,' Stéphanie replied. 'Truly, I am.'

'It's OK, it was an accident. But do look what you're doing

next time. You don't want to take out the whole side in turn!'

Grizel, being Grizel, could not resist being slightly admonitory, despite the fact that she recognised a genuine accident. It could still have been avoided had Stéphanie been a bit more careful, and Grizel, whose hand was actually quite painful despite her brave words, felt sore at not being able to learn the rest of the dance there and then.

'Miss Durrant, may I go and put my hand under the cold tap in the Splashery?'

'Yes, of course. Come back as soon as you can, as you can still learn by watching. Now girls, let's try again. And pay attention to your stick and your partner's stick. I don't want any more accidents!'

They started again, and this time completed the round more successfully. With Grizel out of the dance, the rest of the girls could make up two sets and practise uninterrupted, without having to pause to give a turn to the extra girl sitting on the sidelines. Time was beginning to grow short, and this would allow all the girls a better chance to learn the movements before the lesson ended.

Hot and breathless, they threw themselves into the dance one last time. Once to yourself, Half rounds, Cross over, Back-to-back and Whole-hey were no problem to them, as they knew these patterns already. Interspersed between the verses now came the dib and strike movement and by the third chorus they looked almost professional as they dibbed with vim and struck with vigour. The clashes of the sticks added extra interest to the dance, as they emphasised the beat, and the girls were thoroughly enjoying themselves.

At the end of the lesson, they clamoured for more stick dances.

'That was simply *glorious*,' proclaimed Mary. 'Are there any more like it?'

'Plenty!' laughed Miss Durrant. 'There's "Constant Billy" and "Rodney", but I think,' she added judicially, 'that we should learn another hankie dance first. "Country Gardens" is very pretty, and has some hand clapping in it.'

'Is it anything like the version we know already as a country dance?' asked Rosalie.

'It dances to the same tune, but that is where the similarity ends: there's no clapping in the country dance we do, as you know.'

'It would be nice to dance these dances wearing bells,' remarked Luigia, wistfully. 'Miss Durrant, could we possibly have bells to wear if we dance these at the folk festival?'

'I don't see why not. We can easily attach bells to your shoes using elastic, after all. I shall write to the English Folk Song Society in London, and see if they can recommend a company who will be able to send the bells across.' She nodded. 'Be warned, though. I shall only let you dance with bells on at the festival if you can all jingle in time. There are few things that sound worse than a morris side in which the bells do not ring in time. It is scrappy and unprofessional to watch and to listen to.'

'That doesn't leave us long to learn how to jingle in time,' mused Juliet. 'Still, with some practice and application, I am sure we can manage it. Thank you Miss Durrant.'

Miss Durrant smiled at them. 'Now girls, it's nearly time for *Kaffee und Kuchen*, so you need to hurry if you're not going to be late. Be gone!'

At *Kaffee und Kuchen*, the Middles and Juniors couldn't help but hear how excited the Seniors were by their new dance. Joey in particular was disgruntled.

'Oh, it isn't fair! I *love* morris dancing, and they're the ones who'll get to dance at the festival, because they'll have had more practice. And to be able to think about *bells*, too!' she sighed wistfully. 'Still, I suppose I should be glad that I'll be able to watch them dance. An', if we're lucky …'

'… Miss Durrant will teach us a stick dance too!' finished Frieda. 'I am sure, *liebe* Jo, that she will teach us one next week. She perhaps wanted to see how the Seniors got on first. After all, it does sound more difficult than hankies.'

'And one is more exposed to the risk of being hurt,' put in Aurélie, who had heard all about Stéphanie's contretemps with Grizel. '*Pauvre* Stéphanie, she hit Grizel's finger by mistake, and she feels so bad.'

'Not surprised, if Grizel had a temper on her at the time. Is Grizel OK?' put in Joey. 'She won't mind if she can't write, and it would be a positive relief not to be able to play the piano for a while, but can you imagine if she couldn't play tennis, or cricket, or go boating?'

'I think that she is all right,' answered Aurélie. '*Ma cousine* said that Miss Durrant sent her to the Splasheries to put cold water on her hand, and look, now, she is holding her cup just as well as usual!'

'Well, that's a relief. Even if she couldn't play cricket, she'd make sure that we did. She'd keep wanting us to go and practise while she coached! It's much less fun hearing her yell than it is to play on our own.'

They put their cups on the serving hatch, and departed outside, to enjoy the evening boating from the School's boathouse on the lake. It was Miss Bettany's intention to encourage them to spend as much of their spare time as possible on the water, or indulging in other outdoor pursuits, rather than stewing over their Guide tests. This plan was having a positive effect already; Joey was sleeping much better at night, and was less inclined to be snappish. Grizel, too, seemed more settled, while everyone's school work had begun to show a marked improvement in less than a week.

When they did turn themselves over to Guide work, many of the girls found that, despite not having practised Morse, and knots, and flags, and semaphore with the enthusiasm of the first weeks of term, they were still doing better. They were beginning to learn that a stale, tired brain cannot function as well as one that is well rested and well exercised.

It was a relief to be able to sit down by the lake; even in the heat of summer, the waters were cool and clear and refreshing. Some of the younger girls paddled in the shallows; their skirts tucked safely into their knickers to keep them dry, they revelled in the feeling of the pebbles under their bare feet, and hopped from foot to foot as they cooled themselves. Others sat on the landing stage and dangled their legs in the water while they played at cat's cradle, or with their paper dolls, relics of a collection that had belonged to Simone the previous year.

The older girls were allowed to boat or bathe, provided that they were able to swim to the satisfaction of Miss Bettany, and that there was a mistress on duty in case anyone should get into trouble. Madge Bettany had a theory that the girls did best if they were trusted, rather than watched continually, but she also had a duty to her charges, and needed to make sure they were safe. The mistress on duty generally let the girls do as they wished, only interfering if danger presented itself.

'Hi, Stéphanie!' called Grizel, seeing the French girl walking down towards the Chalet's landing stage. 'Come on! If you're quick, there's enough space for one more!'

The French girl hurried down the slope, her blonde plaits flying out behind her, and she fetched up next to the boat and slipped in.

'But your finger, Grizel?'

'Oh, it's fine! I was more surprised than anything else. I'm sorry if I snapped. I was worried that I might not be able to boat, or play cricket, or anything like that!'

'Or play the piano,' put in Joey, wickedly, from her position at the other oar.

'Nope. That I wasn't worried about. A week off from Mademoiselle supervising and Herr Anserl teaching would have been quite restful. Hop in. If we don't push off now, then we won't all get a turn!'

Stéphanie did as she was told; she was grateful to be asked, as she found that her Patrol Leader, Grizel, could be somewhat sharp and unpredictable at times, and she never knew quite where she stood. Grizel, however, was feeling guilty about her earlier reaction, and was determined to make amends and be more of a sister and friend to her fellow-Cornflower.

Stéphanie undid the rope and helped push the boat away from the landing-stage, before settling back to enjoy the peace of the water. It was lovely to be at school here: the lake shone like a blue jewel, and the mountains reflected in it were awe-inspiring in their beauty. A sensitive girl, she would have revelled in her surroundings, were it not for the reason that she was there. Her beloved mother was desperately ill. Stéphanie lived with the heavy knowledge that, without warning, she could be called up to the Sonnalpe to say good-bye. She trailed her hand in the water, and listened to her companions' chatter, silent with her thoughts.

Chapter XIII

Madame Pagnol

The hot weather continued without a break, leaving both staff and pupils feeling tired and lethargic. Even with all the windows wide open, it was well-nigh impossible to sleep throughout the night, and the broken nights soon began to tell on various members of the School. Staff and pupils lived for the evenings, when they could bathe and boat on the lake, as, apart from their morning baths in icy mountain water, it was the only time of day that they felt cool. By mid-June, even Madame herself was privately bemoaning the lack of a camping permit that would have allowed her to take the Guides of the school for a few nights in the cool, shady pine-woods.

'How long is this sticky weather likely to continue?' asked Matron of her colleagues, as they sat outside after the girls had gone to bed, enjoying the novelty of a slight breeze in the darkness. 'I've never known anything like this before!' She fanned herself feebly, before sitting up and unpinning her starched cap, which had been drooping forlornly for much of the day. Shaking out her curls, she relaxed as the breeze penetrated through to her scalp, bringing some much-needed respite.

'Not long, I think,' replied Miss Maynard. 'The wireless said that we can expect something extra in the way of storms in the next few days.'

'Nothing like last term's effort, I hope! We've only just had the fence repaired after it got washed away so thoroughly,' remarked Madge.

'Washed away?' inquired Miss Carthew, distinctly worried by this description. Although an able swimmer, she was not fond of water generally, and she found the idea of a flood of such force as to wash away the strong withe fence quite terrifying.

'Do not look so worried, my dear,' replied Mademoiselle, patting her hand soothingly. 'The fence of which Miss Maynard speaks was much weaker than that which we have now. It had only wooden staves where we now have staves of iron, *n'est-ce pas*?'

'Yes, and the withes are double-laced too,' answered Miss Bettany. 'There really is nothing to worry about any more, particularly since Herr Braun had the ditch built—or rather dug—to carry away any water that might run down from the mountain. It was a "whanger" of a flood, though!' and she chuckled at the memory of Joey's graphic description. 'Do you remember how Evadne suggested that it was similar in scale to the Mississippi bursting its banks, and that we should all climb up on to the roof?'

'It wasn't necessary, though,' broke in Miss Durrant. 'Even at the Kron Prinz Karl, which was affected far worse than we, they didn't need to go romping over the rooftops! We were never in any real danger, but it was devastating to watch all the same. The water swirled up so quickly. Poor Miss Denny was quite terrified, and Mr Denny had us all singing to keep up our spirits.'

The breeze had died down by now, and an almost eerie stillness prevailed. With one accord, the staff agreed that it was time to turn in, and, stacking their folding chairs in the shelter of the eaves at one end of the Chalet, they headed for bed.

Looking out of the window of her small room in Le Petit Chalet as she plaited her long, dark hair, Miss Carthew felt distinctly uneasy. Although the valley was clearly lit by the full moon, and there was no sign of cloud, her compeers' conversation had slightly unnerved her. Sighing, she turned away from the window, and dropped briefly to her knees to pray that the night would be uninterrupted by thunder. Her prayers were answered, but she passed a restless night nevertheless, and appeared at breakfast the next morning looking somewhat pale and wan.

'Did you not sleep well, *ma chérie*?' inquired Mademoiselle, who also slept in Le Petit Chalet, as she poured her colleague a third cup of milky coffee.

'Well enough,' Miss Carthew replied shortly, wondering if she looked as whey-faced as she felt.

Already the day had proved trying, with one or two of the younger girls inclined to be fractious, while Amy Stevens had refused all offers of help with her hair, and was as a result sporting a parting which was not remotely straight, with pigtails that twisted and turned like corkscrews. The mistress sipped her coffee and tried to think herself into a more placid state of mind, reminding herself that Amy was a Brownie, and that plaiting her own hair was one of the things that she needed to be able to do. Still, Miss Carthew felt that it was a mistake to try and practise this in the rush of a weekday morning.

Mademoiselle remained silent, and hoped that her colleague's mood would lift before too long. Fortunately, it was a Wednesday, which meant that Mr Denny would come down from the Sonnenscheinspitze for the afternoon's singing lesson, and that would free Miss Carthew from teaching and allow her to rest for a while. The weather had not broken as Miss Maynard had predicted the previous night, and everyone's temper was beginning to fray as the heat continued unabated. Even Rufus was unsettled, and paced unceasingly round the wood-shed when he was not allowed out for his walks.

Over at the main school building, as they assembled for their first lessons, the girls were also feeling the effects of the hot weather. Joey was suffering from the after-effects of a sleep-deprived night and had snapped violently at Simone as the latter had tried to help her with her books, causing the French child's bottom lip to wobble dangerously while her eyes began to brim over with tears, thus provoking the usual exasperation in Joey.

'It's enough to try the patience of a seraphim, your constant blubbering!' she grumbled unfairly, snatching her books out of Simone's hands, as a particularly big tear splashed on to the cover of her history book, landing in the middle of her inked name, neatly written only the day before, and smearing it messily. 'Oh, do dry up, Simone. Here, use my hanky.'

Ruffled as she was, Joey did not want Miss Carthew to find Simone in such a state, since that would surely result in a series of tiresome questions and the loss of half the lesson, and they had reached an especially interesting point in their study of the Emperor Charlemagne. Joey was keen on history above all other subjects, and she particularly enjoyed her lessons with the new mistress, since she had exhausted most of her sister's knowledge of the subject long ago. Moreover, she was tender-hearted, and although she might find Simone's behaviour exasperating she genuinely did not like to see her chum upset.

From the way that Miss Carthew put her books down on the desk, however, it was evident that the new mistress was as irritable as the rest of the class, and that fireworks were bound to result. To begin with, she was far from pleased to find the girls gathered round Simone instead of being in their seats as they should have been.

Joey heaved a deep sigh as she realised that Simone was *still* leaking tears, and that explanations were bound to be demanded as to why this was, and thus drew the mistress's attention on herself.

'Tired, Joey?' asked the history mistress. 'Or do you have a headache?'

'No, Miss Carthew,' Jo replied, turning to face the mistress.

'Then kindly do not make such asinine noises. There is no call for them.' Miss Carthew's tone was most decidedly clipped. Her mood had not improved with the third cup of coffee, and she was in no frame of mind to look kindly on even the most minor of transgressions. 'Girls, sit down at once, and turn to page— Simone, have you been crying? I had been told that you had managed to grow out of that habit.'

Although she did not mean to be stern, the look that she cast at Simone prompted the girl to burst into noisy sobs again, interspersed with incoherent noises that could have meant anything. The other girls scattered hastily to their places, and Miss Carthew took a deep, steadying breath, prompting Joey to mutter to Evadne, sitting on her left, that if her sigh had been asinine, then Carty's was positively elephantine. This witticism was too much for Evadne, who promptly dissolved into giggles. A hasty application of her fist to her mouth did little to smother them, and the mistress glared at her.

'Kindly stop making that *ridiculous* noise, and remove your hand from your mouth. If you are unable to sit properly, I shall make you stand at the front of the classroom for the rest of the lesson.'

Thus admonished, Evadne contrived to control her fit, and sat primly in her seat, as though she were a heroine in a Victorian novelette.

Satisfied that order had been restored, Miss Carthew returned her attention to Simone, walking over to her and questioning her with what patience she could muster. She was unable to get anything coherent out of her, despite the efforts the girl was making to quell her tears, so she passed over her handkerchief and stalked to the front of the classroom.

'Are any of you able to tell me why Simone is behaving in this way?'

By now, the mistress was feeling thoroughly ruffled, and her patience was wearing extremely thin. She had hoped that she would be able to conduct the lesson without anything untoward occurring. Clearly this was not to be the case.

'Anyone? Come now. At least one of you must know something about it.'

The class sat stony faced, unwilling to say anything; most of them had no idea why Simone was in such a state, although one or two of them were able to hazard the guess that she had had some kind of disagreement with Joey. Those who did know about the disagreement that had occurred a bare fifteen minutes earlier were distinctly disinclined to say anything on the subject, as that would be akin to sneaking on Joey. That young lady was wriggling uneasily in her seat. She knew she was to blame for Simone's outburst, but Miss Carthew's manner did not encourage her to speak up and confess to her misdemeanour.

An incoherent noise from Simone distracted Miss Carthew's attention from the rest of the class.

'What is it now, Simone?' she demanded, her exasperation evident even to Simone.

'*J'ai dit que je pense que j'ai mal*,' sobbed Simone indistinctly. The fact that she was holding the handkerchief tightly pressed to her mouth did nothing to enhance the clarity of her words, and it took the mistress some moments to work out what her pupil had said.

'Ill?' she asked, eventually. 'Why?' and she pressed a cool hand to her pupil's hot forehead to ascertain whether the girl had a temperature. 'Evadne, please go and fetch Matron. Quickly. We haven't got all day for you to spend shilly-shallying around. *Dis-moi*,' turning back to Simone, '*comment as-tu mal?*'

The official language of the Chalet School was English, but all the mistresses spoke both French and German fluently, and at times such as now it was prudent to use their pupil's mother tongue.

'*J'ai mal à la tête!*' sobbed Simone, who was feeling thoroughly wrung out by this point.

'I'm not surprised you've got a headache, with all that crying!' retorted the mistress. Almost immediately she regretted her harsh response, and continued more gently. 'Lay your head down on the desk, and sit quietly until Matron comes. Would you like a glass of water?' Simone nodded feebly. 'Joey, go and ask Marie for some iced water. Bring it straight back. The rest of you, turn to page eighty-six, and make notes on Charlemagne's diplomacy, bearing in mind what we discussed during your last lesson.'

It was not long before Matron appeared, and she bore away the still-subdued Simone to the school's little san, there to spend the rest of the morning in bed and, it was to be hoped, asleep. Wisely, Miss Carthew did not investigate the incident any further; she could tell that there was little to be gained from interrogating the class as to why Simone had been behaving in a manner which was, in fact, relatively normal for her. Although the French girl had made great progress in checking her tendency to tears, she still failed occasionally, and the hot weather combined with the oppressive air pressure was enough to make anyone out of sorts. The mistress sat down at her desk with the iced water that Simone had left behind, and composed her thoughts.

The Middles looked up at her as she replaced the glass slightly clumsily. Thoroughly bored by the departure from her normal manner of teaching, they were easily distracted from their task; no text book could be as stimulating as the discussions they usually enjoyed. Looking back, Miss Carthew motioned them to continue with their work. Evadne opened her mouth to object and closed it again rapidly, since the mistress was determined to enjoy the respite afforded her by the silently working girls, and had glared at her once more. When the bell came for the end of the lesson, the girls were stunned to see their mistress walk out of the room without bothering to set them any preparation. This was a relief; the less time that they spent in the hot classroom in the evening, the better, they considered.

Meanwhile, the Seniors were finding it equally difficult to concentrate on one of Miss Bettany's famous Shakespearean lectures. This was surprising, as her talks were both interesting and stimulating. The unrest among the Seniors stemmed from something more serious than the stultifying weather, however.

The previous Sunday evening, Stéphanie had returned from her weekly visit to her mother in a distinctly troubled state of mind. The hot weather had told on her mother's constitution, and the doctors had told her that they were worried about her recent lack of progress. Even though it was far cooler up on the Sonnalpe than on the lakeside, the continuous, oppressive heat had contributed to Stéphanie's fear that she might lose her mother at any moment. The girl was suffering no illusions regarding the seriousness of her mother's condition, and she knew that her mother probably would not 'get well'. She did not like to think what might happen next, but her imagination had been working hard while she, too, had lain awake the night before. She had confided in Grizel about her fears, and the elder girl had done her best to allay them. Grizel, mindful of her responsibilities as Stéphanie's Patrol Leader, had also told the rest of the Seniors enough for Stéphanie to know that she had only to ask, and she would be able to find comfort from any of her classmates. At times like this, the School's policy was to be as gentle as possible to the girl in question, without hanging round her or 'anything silly like that', as Miss Bettany decreed, and this worked very well.

The whole, class, therefore, knew that Stéphanie was feeling particularly worried that week, and they had done their best to encourage her. All the Seniors remembered Madame Pagnol in their prayers as a matter of course, and several thought of Stéphanie as well, praying that she would receive strength and courage to guide her through the difficult period she was experiencing. Miss Bettany, too, knew that Madame Pagnol's condition was very serious, and she realised that the class's restlessness was due in part to this. She put down her notes, and gazed at the group in front of her, lifting the hair coiled at the nape of her neck as she did so. The reprieve gained was negligible, and she dropped down her hand, resting it on the desk.

'Have any of you really been paying attention to what I've been saying? Can any of you tell me what I have just said?'

The class, like the Middles, were somewhat stupefied by the heat, and, even if they had not been preoccupied by thoughts of Stéphanie's mother, they would not have felt inclined to pay attention to the lecture. Fascinating though the antics of Beatrice and Benedick were in normal weather, the effort of understanding Shakespearean English in these conditions was further compounded for half the class, since English was not their mother tongue. Of the three English girls, Grizel was something of a philistine, and found even Miss Bettany's best lectures trying, as she simply was not interested in Shakespeare's archaic language; while Rosalie and Mary, although both diligent workers, were on the prosaic side when it came to the study of 'the Bard'. However, Mary, a student with a gift for language, was able to answer Miss Bettany's question; although the beauty of the story did not hold her in thrall, the manner in which Shakespeare manipulated the words within that story was fascinating to her.

'In Shakespeare, women are very frequently the doers and inspirers of action,' replied Mary, sounding slightly put out to find herself a lone voice. The rest of the class might well have been thinking about other things, but during study hours she would do her best to pay attention to the matter in hand. She frowned, but was cheered by the smile that Miss Bettany directed at her.

'Well done, Mary. Can anyone else tell me about any of the other points I've made?' she asked, moving round the desk to perch on the edge of it. Seeing Grizel looking completely bewildered, she continued, 'I realise that, on the face of it, that is a silly question; but I want to find out what you think about what I've been saying. Stéphanie, have you any ideas?'

Stéphanie shook her head mutely, and looked as though she might follow her younger compatriot's example by bursting into tears. She had understood very little of Miss Bettany's lecture, and had found the experience immensely frustrating. She was spared the agony of having to think of an answer by a knock at the door.

'Come in!' called the Headmistress; but the door was open before she had completed the phrase.

Mademoiselle stood on the threshold, her kindly face creased in worry.

'Please excuse me, Madame, but I have urgent news. For Stéphanie.'

She crossed the room towards the French girl, and laid her hand over hers. Stéphanie looked up at her, panic making her feel ill inside.

'*Qu'est-ce que c'est? Est-ce que c'est ma mère?*' she asked, her terror clearly visible as what little colour she had drained from her face.

'*Oui. Ta mère a besoin de toi, ma petite.* You must go at once to the Sonnalpe. *Monsieur le docteur Russell ira avec toi, et il va t'expliquer.*'

Mademoiselle turned to her colleague, who nodded permission, and gestured to Stéphanie to leave with her fellow-countrywoman.

They hurried out of the formroom, and Mademoiselle led the girl upstairs to pack a small bag and change into her walking boots. In the meantime, Miss Bettany turned to the twelve remaining girls.

'Let us pray,' she said quietly, 'that Madame Pagnol will have the strength to face whatever may lie before her with dignity and with courage; and that if she must suffer, it should be briefly and with the least possible pain. I am sure you all know how ill she has been, and I know that I can rely on you to all be a friend to Stéphanie, however she might need you. Yes, Grizel?'

'Please may I go to say good-bye to her? And to let her know that we're thinking about her, and praying?' Grizel asked.

This was a most unusual request for the girl who, as a rule, thought of herself first. When she had been a small child, her own mother had died after a long illness, and Miss Bettany recognised that Grizel would be able to offer Stéphanie something greater than sympathy: insight. She silently gave thanks that, this term, Grizel was apparently benefiting from Guides, and learning to look beyond herself.

'Yes, you may. Stay for a few moments while we pray together, and then go and wait for her in the front hall. Please tell her that I'll be there shortly.'

The girls bowed their heads, and prayed fiercely in silence for a minute or so, before Grizel, at a nod from the mistress, slipped out of the room to wait in the hall, ready to support her friend to the best of her abilities.

Chapter XIV

A Long Night

When she came to look back on it, and to remember that dreadful night when her mother had hung on a knife-edge between life and death, it appeared to Stéphanie that no other night could ever last so long. It was Midsummer's Eve, and the daylight remained until twenty-two o'clock, while the night fell for only a few short hours, with sunrise at half-past four the next morning. The heat on the Sonnalpe was much less oppressive than in the valley, but it seemed to the weary girl that she could not remember how a cool breeze felt, much less how it was to be comfortable. She was hot and sticky with the effort of the long climb up the alpe, and had only paused to wash her hands and face before she went to sit with her mother.

At around three in the morning, the weather finally broke with a thunderstorm that rolled around the valley for hours on end. Down by the lakeside, Rufus howled with pent-up tension. Stéphanie's overstrung nerves almost reached breaking point, and she cried aloud at the first roll of thunder, before realising that it was only a storm. Her mother lay senseless, not noticing as her daughter dropped her hand and sped to the window.

Stéphanie had refused to leave her mother's side once she had completed the long climb up from the lakeside, and Dr Russell had allowed her to remain in the room even while he and the nurse strove to alleviate Madame Pagnol's breathlessness. Miss Bettany, who had accompanied the girl, had perforce to wait elsewhere in the chalet, as the room was small, and there was not enough space for everyone.

At around midnight the point came when the doctor knew that they could do no more, and Stéphanie was left with her mother, with the nurse and Miss Bettany for company. Dr Russell would have preferred the girl to get some sleep on the bed which had been set up for her in the next room, but she was adamant that she must stay with her mother. As he said to the nurse:

'For now, Madame Pagnol is Stéphanie's world. If this is the end, and it could very well be, it will be an immense comfort to Stéphanie in later years to know that she was with her mother.'

Nurse had concurred.

'*Das stimmt.* There has been no word from *Capitaine de frégate* Pagnol's ship?'

'None at all, I'm afraid. No-one seems to know where it might be, and that's making any kind of contact awfully difficult …' He tailed off, leaving unspoken his belief that *le capitaine* would only hear of his wife's deterioration after her death.

'Quite,' replied Nurse briskly. 'Shall I ask the maid to bring a tray to Stéphanie in Madame Pagnol's room?'

'Yes, I think that would be best—and one for Fräulein Bettany, also. Stéphanie understands that she will not be allowed to remain there unless she eats all the food that we bring her, and she has the reclining chair so that she can try to get some proper rest. And Fräulein Bettany will be with her while I am away. Please make sure that Stéphanie does eat the food. I don't want her to become ill too. She may need all her resources.'

With which utterance he nodded to Nurse, and departed to his own chalet to make a further attempt to get in touch with *le capitaine*, only to be told once again that the ship was apparently out of radio contact and that no-one could be sure exactly when this would be restored.

There was nothing to be done, so Dr Russell, concerned for

his patient, lost no time in returning to Madame Pagnol's chalet, arriving just as the storm broke.

Gazing out of the window, Stéphanie barely noticed the amazing spectacle that nature was putting on. After the first crash of thunder had roused her from her vigil by her mother's bed, she had gone to the window, not really thinking about what she was doing. As a child growing up in the Midi, she had always adored watching the thunderstorms that had punctuated the summer months like so many performances of the 1812 Overture. The combination of thunder, lightning and rain had completely exhilarated her, and made her feel more at one with her surroundings than any amount of chasing butterflies, clambering over rocks and poking around in the fine, dry soil that collected in their crevices ever could have done. Now, preoccupied with her thoughts, she gazed unseeing as the thunder rolled round the lake, interrupted by the occasional flash of lightning, for almost an hour before the rain finally came. Almost immediately, the fuggy, sticky feeling in the air disappeared and, as the rain grew harder, the storm grew stronger, and Stéphanie turned back towards the bed.

Like her daughter, Mme Pagnol was exhilarated by thunderstorms, and Stéphanie was sure that she had roused slightly with the first crash. A startlingly beautiful woman, as fair as her daughter, she had waist-length white-blonde hair and milky-blue eyes, and showed a penchant for flowing clothes like those seen in Pre-Raphaelite paintings. She was Austrian by birth, but had adopted her husband's country with enthusiasm until her illness had forced her to return to her family's homeland. Especially she had loved the French forest in which their house was set, and would ramble there by day and by night in all weathers, taking her chances against the rain, and crucially weakening her constitution with the constant colds that resulted. Among the sturdy local farm workers she had become something of a legend, and they spoke amongst themselves of '*la folie des Pagnol*', recalling an occasion when she had been glimpsed during a midnight storm, a ghostly apparition in her flowing gown with her glorious hair streaming about her, lit at intervals by lightning.

Stéphanie looked at her mother, and sat down beside the bed again, taking hold of her hand. She was not sure, but she thought that since the rain had begun to fall, her mother's breathing had become less laboured, and far quieter and gentler: it was almost impossible to hear it, and Stéphanie was suddenly terrified. Madame Pagnol's colouring, too, seemed less hectic.

Stéphanie looked at the nurse, who had been sitting knitting something small and white in between checking her patient's pulse and general condition.

'Is she?' she asked tremblingly. 'Is she?'

Her voice rose, and became higher in pitch. She sounded close to tears. Wordlessly, the nurse motioned to her to be quiet, and listened intently to her patient, picking up Madame Pagnol's wrist and checking her pulse. She nodded to herself, her winged cap throwing up strange shadows in the light from the small table lamp. Stéphanie held her breath momentarily, her eyes flicking between the nurse and her mother while the former counted. Letting it out again, she looked at her questioningly.

'Is she?' she asked for a third time.

'Wait. I go for Herr Doktor Russell. I have just now heard him return.' And with this, Nurse swept out of the room, leaving the door open behind her.

Miss Bettany watched her charge anxiously; unable to help the woman on the bed, she prayed as fervently as she had ever prayed in her life.

Stéphanie sat alone by the bedside, feeling as though her heart had leapt out of her chest and into her throat with the express intention of preventing her from breathing. Her stomach clenched and unclenched with fear and hope. She took a deep breath, and leant forward, resting her forearms on her mother's bed. Clasping her hands together, she bowed her head until it touched her hands, and prayed as hard as she could.

'*Ave Maria, gratia plena, dominus tecum.*'

So absorbed was she that she never noticed the nurse's return, with Dr Russell just behind her. He crossed quickly over to the bed, and Stéphanie looked up at him in sheer relief; the few moments alone with her mother had taken more out of her than all the rest of the night. Desperately hoping that she was showing some sign of real improvement, and equally fearful that she was simply rallying for one last time before her death, Stéphanie had felt the time never ending.

Still praying, but under her breath, she stepped back to allow the doctor to examine her mother once more. He worked with the minimum of fuss, and was soon finished, laying down her mother's hand and covering it with his own for a moment before he turned to face the girl.

The thunder continued to roll ominously round the lake, the rain drumming on the rooftop, the occasional droplet splashing through the window into the room.

Jem Russell looked at Stéphanie compassionately while he searched for the right words.

A sudden piercing pain shot through Stéphanie's heart, and her eyes filled with stinging tears, which gradually spilled over and trickled down her cheeks. Her breathing became ragged, her chest heaved, and the room was silent but for the sound of the tempest outside.

'*Je suis desolé*, Stéphanie. I am so very, very sorry.' Dr Jem's voice cracked very slightly on the last word. Although it was not the first time that he had had to break such news, he had not before had to do so to such a young girl.

'Is she in pain?' whispered Stéphanie, her eyes fixed on the figure in the bed, whose breathing was ever slower and shallower.

'No. She has been heavily sedated. She cannot feel any more pain. It will not be long, now, until she is with God. I shall stay with you as long as you both need me.' He laid his hand on her shoulder.

As the sun's milky light began to penetrate the thick clouds that hung over the Sonnalpe, Madame Pagnol gave a gentle sigh and slipped quietly away from her daughter. A bolt of lightning lit up the room, followed seconds later by the loudest crash of thunder yet. The storm was at its height, but suddenly Stéphanie found it almost comforting, remembering how her mother had danced under the raindrops so many times before, and forgetting for the time being the harm that this had done her.

As the nurse began to perform her last duties towards Madame Pagnol and Dr Russell turned to confer with Madge, Stéphanie, desperate for a moment's solitude, slipped out on to the verandah and thence on to the lawn in front of the chalet. Within moments, the girl was soaked to the skin, and she stood there, motionless, before beginning to whirl round and round. Arms outstretched, she twisted and turned until she was dizzy, stumbling several times before falling over on to her hands and knees. Kneeling down, racked with sobs, her head bowed and with her arms wrapped around herself, she gave full force to her anguish. Gradually, her sobs abated, and she cried softly for a while, until at last she sat up and dashed her sleeve across her face. Miss Bettany, who had followed and was now watching her pupil in deep concern, hastened to break the spell.

'Stéphanie?' she called across the grass.

Stéphanie turned her head to see her Headmistress standing on the verandah.

'*Madame? Attendez. Je viens.*'

Stéphanie turned her head, and looked out over the shelf to the mountains opposite, the lightning flashing above them, the forbidding peaks black against the dark grey clouds. She silently prayed for strength before getting up and crossing the grass to her Headmistress.

'Come, and let me find you some dry clothes, *ma petite*. You are very wet.'

Miss Bettany looked at her pupil with compassion. Stéphanie's face plainly showed the strain she had been under for the past few days, the dark shadows under her eyes told of many sleepless nights and her Headmistress's heart went out to her. She held out her hand as the girl walked towards her. Ignoring Stéphanie's bedraggled state, she put a comforting arm round her shoulders as they walked back into the house. There, the girl was subjected to a hot bath and provided with a mug of hot milk to stave off any chance of illness. She was sure that she would not be able to sleep, but the tiny dose which the doctor had slipped into her mug soon took effect, and she slept the clock round, and awoke the next morning feeling refreshed, despite the sharp pain that pierced her heart.

Chapter XV

Contemplation

Stéphanie returned to school within a week of her mother's death. Her father could not as yet be contacted, and her aunt agreed that it was better for her to be with the other girls. She spent a great deal of time with her cousin Aurélie, who perhaps understood better than any of the other girls the strain she had been under, and who missed her Tante Augustine greatly. The two cousins had grown up together, and each knew well how the other felt and was thinking.

As Stéphanie did not return to lessons immediately, and Aurélie was one of the younger Middles, it was easy enough for them to spend time together without necessitating too many special arrangements. The School already took care of two girls who were motherless, and the staff were practised in providing the help and encouragement that Juliet and the Robin needed. Grizel too, with her difficult relationship with her stepmother, had found, since the death of her Grannie the previous term, that the School looked after more than just her physical needs.

The aunt with whom Stéphanie had been staying had been very warm and welcoming, but she had always felt herself something of an outsider. Brought up in France as she had been, she was far from fluent in her mother's language, and although her German had improved greatly during the few weeks she had spent in Austria, it was nowhere near good enough to provide her with an understanding of the subtle nuances that she needed to deal with the current situation. Moreover, since her linguistic ability had been born of necessity, rather than desire, and from the time of her mother's death that need had been inextricably tangled with a sense of loss that seemed almost tangible in its desolation, she had found it harder than ever to speak the language and frequently found herself unable to compose even the simplest phrases.

At the Chalet School, however, in addition to the extremely comforting presence of Madame, there were enough French girls to allow her to convey how she felt and, more importantly, what she wanted from her friends with the minimum of fuss. The advantage brought by a shared native language at such moments was immense. The Robin, in particular, was deeply comforting, offering such tokens of affection as she was allowed, often accompanied by a murmur of '*Pauvre Stéphanie!*' whenever they met. It was often said that there was nothing quite so consoling as the School baby, who had met with nothing but loving tenderness all her life, and, thus equipped, treated everyone the same way.

In addition to Mademoiselle, Aurélie and Simone, Stéphanie was part of a group of schoolgirls who, as well as sympathising deeply with her loss, were possessed of sufficient ability at French to be understanding even when Stéphanie's command of German or English had completely deserted her. Joey spoke French almost as well as a native, and the Seniors had greatly improved in languages over the year that most of them had spent at the school. All spoke French, English and German well; and some took Italian conversation classes with Miss Denny, who visited the school as frequently as her brother.

Even Grizel was able, by now, to speak French fluently enough for Stéphanie to be able to speak intimately to her without worrying that her sentences might be misconstrued. The two girls fell into such a conversation by chance, one afternoon early in the week after Madame Pagnol's funeral, as they lazed around in deckchairs during their afternoon rest. The entire discussion took place in French.

'Do you think of your mother, still?' asked Stéphanie presently. She was desperate to talk to someone who had experienced a similar loss, and was drawn to Grizel as her Patrol Leader, although Grizel was not always the most understanding of girls. The Robin was too young to talk to, and Miss Bettany was often pressed for time, although she did her best by the girl.

'Sometimes,' replied Grizel. 'I hadn't really thought about it—about how often I think about her, I mean.'

Stéphanie nodded; convoluted though the sentence was, she understood what the elder girl was trying to say.

'I suppose—' Grizel faltered, and then fell silent.

A few moments passed, during which the enchanting song of a thrush could be heard from the direction of the tennis court. Stéphanie cocked her head appreciatively as she listened to its rippling notes. Nature's beauty had always moved her, and she blinked furiously to prevent the now familiar welling-up feeling, as though her heart was trying to break out of her throat, from turning into a fresh effusion of tears. Although she understood that it 'wasn't done' to burst into tears at the drop of a hat, she did not yet realise that, under certain extenuating circumstances, it was perfectly understandable and permissible that she might feel this way.

Grizel bit her lip and flushed slightly before continuing. Facing the death of the mother of a member of her patrol was a disconcerting experience, prompting her to re-examine her feelings about her own mother's death some ten years earlier.

'I suppose I don't think about her as much as you think about yours; and I'm not sure I ever would have. It all happened so long ago. I hadn't had her for my own as long as you've had your mother; I was very young at the time.'

Grizel struggled. She would really much rather that Juliet or Madame spoke with Stéphanie and helped her. It was not in her nature to think deeply about such matters, and she had not the instinctive in-built sympathy of the Robin: it took effort to work out the best way to help her friend. However, she recognised her responsibility to be both a sister and a friend to her fellow-Guide, and accordingly steeled herself to the effort.

'And you can't remember what you felt then?' Stéphanie desperately wanted to know that the way she was feeling was not only usual, given the circumstances, but that it was transient. Many of the things that had previously brought only joy to her now brought, if not pain exactly, then deepest melancholy.

'I felt—' Grizel paused, as she was finding the conversation extremely hard going and would have done even if she had not been speaking French. 'I felt sad, and lonely, and confused. Everyone around was very upset, and trying not to let me see that, and I could tell that something was very wrong. No-one really had any time for *me*.'

A fleeting expression crossed her pretty face, and for a moment she resembled a small, sulky child. Grizel's mother had been a semi-invalid following the birth of her only baby, and Grizel's memories of her consisted chiefly of a pale, wan figure occupying a chaise-longue, repeatedly asking her small daughter in a whining tone to 'play more quietly' if she wished to stay in the same room, or else risk banishment to the small, rather gloomy day-nursery.

Rousing herself, Grizel continued.

'But then, I don't really think that anyone had much time for me anyhow. Not until I went to live with Grannie.'

'But how long did that feeling last?' persisted poor Stéphanie. 'I mean, you don't look particularly confused or lost now!'

'Only until I went to live with Grannie,' replied Grizel, who was rather more confused about her own feelings at this point than she had been for quite some time, as tends to happen when one suddenly goes in for a bout of self-reflection after years of not really bothering to think at all. 'Father had decided to take off and work overseas, so I didn't really see anything of him for years—until he came back and presented me to his new wife. He got married on my tenth birthday, you know. And she wasn't really expecting a new daughter as well as a new husband. That's beside the point, though. The thing is, when I got to Grannie's, there was enough time for her to explain everything to me. And she fussed over me, and petted me—Miss Bettany probably thinks she did too much of that—' with an insight surprising in one usually so careless—'and made it all seem, well,' glancing round to check that there were no prefects in earshot, and thus that she could get away with using slang, 'OK again.'

'So you didn't really realise what you'd lost?'

'No, not really. If you asked Joey, I bet she'd say the same sort of thing. Her mother died when she was just a baby, and then Madame's been as much of a mother as a sister to her ever since. Juliet too—her parents behaved as if they hated her, and she didn't think much of them! Why, I remember when I first saw her mother, I thought she must be her stepmother. Poor Ju, all her mother seemed to do was scold her!'

Stéphanie pondered this for a while. It occurred to her that, if Madame had been like a mother to Joey, thus alleviating Joey's own sense of loss, then Madame must have been close to Stéphanie's own age when she'd been orphaned. However, if Joey was now thirteen, that would make Madame almost thirty—and she certainly didn't look as old as that. On occasion, she seemed far more like an older sister than a Headmistress. However, on the morning after that dreadful night, she had been so very tender, and had seemed to know exactly how Stéphanie felt; as though she were exactly Stéphanie's age but at the same time more grown-up.

Thoroughly confused by the path her thoughts were taking, Stéphanie changed the subject with a jolt.

'What happened at Guides this week?' she asked.

She had been too upset to attend, feeling unable to face the well-meaning sympathy of the School *en masse*, and instead had spent the morning alternately trying to finish the embroidered tray-cloth she had been making for her mother, and reading and re-reading the same page of a translation of *Pride and Prejudice*. Many tears were wept over that scrap of cloth, but at the time it had seemed to Stéphanie that it would be a great pity not to try and finish it, since there was so little left to do before it was complete. In fact, had her mother not died, it would probably have been finished and presented to her by now.

Grizel looked at Stéphanie in surprise, before regaining her customary aplomb.

'Oh, the usual things.'

Stéphanie raised her pale eyebrows questioningly, making her periwinkle-blue eyes look even larger than usual.

'Well, we had drill, did yet *more* Morse practice, and then played a game which was all about National Emblems; Captain called out the names of the emblems, and we had to sort through a pile of slips that had been put on a chair at the end of the room—the other end of the room from where all the patrols were lined up, silly—and find the country that went with the emblem. You got a point for getting the right country, and another for being the first patrol back to the Captain with the right answer.'

'Who won?'

'Poppies, I think. Yes, Mary Burnett's such a swot, she knew all of the answers without having to think at all. Takes me all my time to learn even one of those sorts of things. Your cousin Aurélie was very good, too—she's a fast runner, and I think she'll make a good cricketer when she's a little older.'

'And the Brownies?'

'They made dolls' cradles out of scraps of cloth and old matchboxes. I think that Herr Braun had collected the boxes up for them. The Robin showed me hers, and it was quite good for such a kid.'

The conversation turned towards Guides in general; the last uniforms had arrived from London the week before, and the whole company now had the full uniform of long blue jumper, navy skirt, yellow tie, broad-brimmed hat and, in the case of the Patrol Leaders, lanyards. As Joey had remarked, on seeing the whole company in uniform, they really looked like Guides. Evadne was heard to say that, once she had her uniform, she *felt* like a Guide, and was promptly reminded by a passing prefect that it wasn't the Uniform that made the Guide, but the Guide that makes the Uniform—effectively squashing her for a few minutes.

As the afternoon wore on, both Grizel and Stéphanie grew drowsy, and by the time the bell rang for *Kaffee und Kuchen* both had fallen asleep in their chairs. The hot, milky coffee revived them somewhat, and after the meal was over, Grizel went off to make up a tennis four with Gisela, Gertrud and Juliet, while Stéphanie sought out Madame, to see if there was any news from her father.

Every day between seventeen and nineteen o'clock Madge made sure she was in her little room, ready to see anyone who wished it. It was well known throughout the school that anyone who wished to see her, from Gisela down to little Amy Stevens and the Robin, could go at that time, and be assured of her undivided attention. Most frequently, Madge found herself the recipient of a tender hug and kiss from the Robin, or a whirlwind visit from Joey, en route from her *Kaffee und Kuchen* to some activity with her friends, or perhaps piano practice. On other occasions, Grizel would drop in, with yet another unfeasible plan for the school to take part in matches with one or another part of the local community.

Stéphanie knocked timidly at the slightly open door. She waited, her breathing shallow and fast.

'Come in!' called Miss Bettany.

Stéphanie stepped into the room, her brows furrowed and her eyes questioning.

'Is there any news?' she asked, without waiting to waste time on mere pleasantries. 'Have you found my father? Where is he? When will he be back?'

Miss Bettany gazed compassionately at her pupil. Every day for the past fortnight, Stéphanie had been the first pupil to arrive at her room at the appointed time. On more than one occasion, she had been waiting patiently outside for her Headmistress to return from her own *Kaffee und Kuchen*. Every day, Miss Bettany had had to disappoint her again by announcing gently that they had still not been able to make contact with *monsieur le capitaine*, but that she was sure that he was safe and well, and that they would find him soon.

'Stéphanie—'

She got no further, as Stéphanie interrupted.

'He is *still* at sea? He is *still* away? Oh! *Why* did he have to go so far away, and for so long? He knew how ill Maman felt! And he left her! He left me!'

The words poured out in a torrent, and she burst into stormy tears. Madge left her chair and walked over to the sobbing girl, taking her in her arms. The continuing absence of news from Stéphanie's father had told on the girl, and she was unable to eat properly. Madge was deeply worried, although she understood much of what Stéphanie felt only too well.

'Stéphanie.'

She paused, but Stéphanie continued to sob heart-brokenly.

'*Stéphanie!* Please stop crying. I know where your father is.'

Slowly, Stéphanie raised a tearful face to look at her.

'I know where your father is,' Miss Bettany repeated. 'He is in Constantinople. His ship came into port last night, and the French Navy has been able to make contact with him at last. They have given him leave on compassionate grounds, and he is on his way here. He sent you a telegram before he left, and it has only just arrived.'

Stéphanie was momentarily speechless. Miss Bettany gently led her across the room to the sofa and bade her sit down, handing her a clean, white handkerchief with which to wipe her swollen eyes, before turning to the desk and picking up the slip of paper. Silently she handed it to Stéphanie, who took it incredulously, holding it as though it was the most precious thing ever created.

'*J'arrive bientôt. Je t'aime. Sois courageuse, mon ange. Papa*,' she read.

For a moment, the awful feeling of loneliness lifted from her heart, and she almost smiled.

'It will be all right now, won't it? Madame? It—it doesn't hurt so much now, I think.'

'Yes, it will be "all right". Not immediately, and not all the time, but little by little, it will be all right,' Madge replied, tenderly stroking Stéphanie's hair. She was struck by the sudden memory of an inspiring sermon that their vicar had given the week before she and Joey had left England for Austria just over a year ago, during which he had spoken of a tract that he had read while at theological college. It had been written by an anchoress, Julian of Norwich, in the Middle Ages, and a phrase from it had stuck in Miss Bettany's mind: 'All shall be well, and all shall be well, and all manner of things shall be well.'

'How can you tell? But you can, can't you?'

Madge nodded.

'Yes, you can,' Stéphanie said to herself, comforted.

They sat in silence for a while, each thinking of her own mother. Madge had been only thirteen years old when her parents had died within a few weeks of each other. The whirlwind removal from India to Cornwall, with Joey only a tiny, frail ten-month-old baby, had occupied all her attention as she had been told that she had to be a mother to Joey, and Dick a father. The two children had focussed all their attention on their younger sister, and their hurt had abated in their absorption.

Stéphanie, mused Madge, had had no such absorbing scrap of humanity to look after, and her grief had turned inwards instead of dispersing. Madge still missed her own mother, but she knew that having to look after Joey had helped her immensely, and she hoped that the return of Stéphanie's father would prove crucial in helping Stéphanie get over her loss.

Chapter XVI

Exams ...

'Quiet please! Settle down and stop fussing. The longer you take to be quiet, the later the exam will start; and I can assure you, if the exam does not start on time, it will not end on time. And if it does not end on time, you will still find that the next exam starts on time, and the time you are wasting now will be taken from your Break.'

The Middles gazed at Miss Maynard in horror and swiftly settled themselves, arranging their pens, pencils and geometry sets with utmost speed. The mathematics examination which faced them was, for the majority, their very first experience of a serious end-of-year exam, and they were well aware that their positions at the end of these exams would not only be recorded on their reports, but could also determine which form they would be in next term.

Even the excitement of attempting their Second Class Guide tests had not entirely distracted their attention from the matter, although maths had seemed rather mundane by comparison; after all, they reasoned, who could be expected to concentrate only upon algebra when they had their heads full of knots and bandages?

Joey had put it best, in her inimitable style, as they lounged in the garden one evening. She had as great an enthusiasm for Guiding as ever, but, still mindful of the events that had led to her being confined to bed earlier in the term, she had learnt how to restrain herself in its application.

'If the maths exam that Maynie sets only has some questions about estimating the height of a tree, then I might just be able to understand trigonometry. As it is, the square on the hypotenuse may be equal to the square of the sum of the other two sides—'

'Joey,' interrupted Margia, who had a much better grasp of the theorem in question, 'it's equal to the sum of the squares on the other two sides. You know that.'

'Is it? Well—it's all the same, anyhow.' Joey dismissed Margia's correction irreverently. 'Point being, that if we had some trees or a river or something like B-P talks about in the handbook when he explains how to estimate heights, then I might just remember it all. Properly.'

Joey's friends had looked at her, surprised. Her abhorrence of maths was well known throughout the Chalet School, and it was rare for her to bring up the subject at all. Knowing how to estimate height and distance was something that would in fact cause Miss Jo a great deal of anxiety when it came to her First Class tests, for the fact remained that mathematics were mathematics, regardless of whether they were applied to Guiding tests or no, and her grasp of the niceties of trigonometry would remain erratic, to say the least. That, however, is a story for another day.

'With the T-square as well?' asked Simone, who was fascinated by that particular gadget, owing, in part, to the description about lifting it to her nose.

'Yes, with the T-square. Although,' and here she consulted her handbook, 'there's no mention of that on this page, and where on earth is one supposed to find a six-foot staff? We don't carry those any more, except for the Patrol Leaders, and their staves have got the patrol flags stuck to them. Still, they would probably do for estimating height. How tall is the parasol?' They were sheltering from the strong sun under one of the School's many parasols, having 'bagged' their particular favourite. 'It would be fun to work out the tree's height.'

Working out the length of the parasol, combined with the pacing to work out the height of the tree, had kept them occupied for the rest of that evening, and had given their brains some mathematical exercise that did, in fact, stand them in good stead for the forthcoming exams. Joey, for one, did not face the paper with quite her usual feeling of trepidation.

'Thank you,' continued Miss Maynard, as the girls finished settling themselves. 'You may not turn over your papers until you each have one in front of you. Once I have let you turn over the papers, you must remain silent until I have collected in the last answer sheet. You may not look at any other book throughout the exam. You are on your honour to look only at your own exam paper, and at no-one else's.'

She looked round at her class, noting her pupils' pallor, then smiled reassuringly.

'Don't worry if there are questions you cannot answer. Read all the exam paper through before you start to answer anything, and answer the question you think you can answer best, first. You'll probably find that once you've answered that one, your brain will be more in the swing of things, and you'll be able to tackle the rest of them. *Aurélie, ne t'inquiètes pas. Ton examen est en français.*' As she spoke, she moved among the girls, distributing exam papers. 'Margia—' in response to a snort from that young woman—'Aurélie's paper is in French because she has only been learning English for a few weeks, and she is already at a disadvantage. And you have a paper in front of you, and must not make a sound.'

Margia shut her mouth, and prepared to turn her attention to her paper. She was not worried about the mathematics examination, as, like many musicians, she had a natural aptitude for the subject. Not so the rest of the class. Joey was already grasping her head as she grappled with algebraic equations, and Miss Maynard knew that by the end of the exam, her hair would be sticking out at all angles.

Suzanne Mercier, too, was most decidedly not gifted at maths, and could feel her grasp of the subject slowly but surely slipping away from her. The day's heat had not yet intensified so much that thinking was impossible, but it was warm enough already to cause an extra strain. Wiping her hand on her summer frock, she grasped her pencil more firmly (she always maintained that she could think better in pencil) and applied herself to reading the paper for a third time, hoping that she could make sense of one of the questions. The two Italians, Giovanna and Bianca, were grappling with two distinctly different methods of calculating the area of a lake, while Cyrilla Maurús's mind had wandered completely away from the subject of walls, and was wondering what lunch would be.

A stifled hiccough from Aurélie quickly brought Cyrilla back to the classroom, if not the wall, and she looked up, concerned. Aurélie sniffed, and rummaged in her pockets for her handkerchief. Extracting a bedraggled piece of lace-edged cloth, she dabbed at her eyes and blew her nose. Miss Maynard raised her eyebrows questioningly at the girl, but she had lowered her head and was glaring at her paper again. The words swam in front of her eyes, and, lowering her head to the desk, she gave up the struggle and began to cry quietly.

'Do you want to leave the room?' asked Miss Maynard, bending over her quietly. Aurélie convulsed slightly, which Miss Maynard interpreted as meaning 'yes'. 'Come along then. It is not so important. Girls,' she continued, raising her voice, 'I am putting you on your honour to remain silent and to continue with your papers.' She did not think it necessary to tell them that they must not compare answers; the whole school had been very impressed by what they had read of the 'English sense of honour' in various stories, and strove to emulate it. Miss Maynard knew that all the girls would work out their own answers, without debating them amongst themselves while she was out of the classroom. With the minimum of fuss, she led Aurélie from the room and took her upstairs to Matron's domain.

In the Fifth form room, Stéphanie was finding it difficult to concentrate on her history paper. Although her attention had been engaged by Miss Carthew's fascinating lessons, the Renaissance period had been entirely unknown to her before her arrival at the school, and the broad strokes with which the mistress had described the interaction between the three 'Renaissance Princes', Henry VIII, Charles V and François IV, were entirely alien to her. Choosing an essay from the selection of titles in front of her, she racked her brains to remember what she'd read about the Field of the Cloth of Gold, and tried to forget that it would still be some days before her father arrived.

In front of her, Grizel scratched her head in thought. Not old enough to put her hair up, she had, for the time being, skewered up her heavy tail of hair using a pencil, and it kept threatening to slide down her back under the furious onslaught to which she was subjecting it. How she wished that she had paid as much attention to her school lessons as she had to the Guide syllabus. After all, she now realised, a Guide surely needed to know about history and calculus as much as about First Aid and cookery. Suppressing the rising bile in her throat, she re-secured her unorthodox hairstyle and, ignoring the glance that Miss Carthew had thrown in her direction, returned to the paper.

The exams continued for several days, with two or three subjects each day. The Seniors were somewhat annoyed by the fact that the Middles' exams only lasted forty-five minutes for every hour that theirs took. However, since the younger girls were made to rest outside in silence while their elders continued to work, the latter were not too greatly affected by the fact that the rest of the school was at liberty.

The Seniors on the whole, Grizel aside, were much less concerned about their examinations. Gisela, Bernhilda and Wanda were all leaving at the end of the term, and the other members of the class felt reasonably confident that they would divide into Sixth and Fifth forms based more upon age than positions in form. They had also adopted a rather more level-headed approach to Guiding. The Honesty patrol had decided early on that they would continue to give the bulk of their time to their duties as Head Girl and prefects, since, as Gisela had said when they held a Patrol Council:

'Our first duty is to the School. And, although we have a duty to do our best as Guides, we have a greater duty to do our best by the Chalet School, since as prefects, we are responsible for the well-being of all.'

'We need to set a good example, and show that, although it is important to play the game as Guides, we cannot allow Guides to prevent us from fulfilling our other obligations properly,' agreed Bernhilda. 'Besides, we shall only be Guides for a term, and we have been prefects for a year already.'

'However,' put in Wanda, her blue eyes glowing, 'we must not forget Guides because of our other duties. There is a lot of good in the Guide movement, I think, and we shall be ambassadors, of a sort, in Austria.'

The other girls had nodded; they were well aware that the Chalet School company was the only British company in Austria. There was in fact only one other company of any description in Austria, run by a Fräulein Hofmann in Vienna; various problems had meant that the movement had not flourished as well there as it had in other parts of the world. Mindful of their duties as prefects, the Honesties, therefore, had not progressed as far with their Second Class as the rest of the company, but nor had their work suffered to the same extent as that of the rest of the School. If anything they, and the remainder of the prefects, had been distracted more by the lively discussions about the forthcoming folk festival, and speculation about who would fill the position of Head Girl after Gisela had left, than by anything else.

The exams still seemed like an eternity, and many were the grumbles among the Middles especially, when it was decreed that no girl would be allowed to open *any* sort of book, including story books, after the last exam of each day was over. Strict supervision had prevented them from opening books for last-minute revision between exams, and one or two had been counting on using the time between *Kaffee und Kuchen* and *Abendessen* to straighten out several facts which were somewhat unclear in their minds. Instead, the Headmistress arranged for them to spend their leisure hours out of doors, in various healthy pursuits.

'We're going swimming?' gasped Joey incredulously, earning herself a sharp rebuke from her sister in front of the entire school during assembly on the second day of exam week.

'Quiet, *please*! Yes, Josephine, you will go swimming instead of studying. It will do you all,' continued Miss Bettany, in a gentler tone, as she gazed at the tired faces in front of her, 'a great deal of good to rest your minds and exercise your bodies instead. Tomorrow we shall hold a tennis tournament, and, on Thursday, we shall have a set of 'Tip-and-Run' cricket matches.'

The school beamed at this prospect; encouraged by Grizel, Tip-and-Run, a version of cricket in which the batsmen *had* to run regardless of how well they had hit the ball, had become a favourite activity amongst the Middles during their spare time.

'It only remains for me to wish you all luck with the rest of your exams. I am sure that you will all do yourselves credit. There are only three more days of them, and none of you have more than three exams in one day; most of you have only two. And, after the exams, I promise you, we shall have some fun.'

Miss Bettany nodded to Mademoiselle at the piano, and she struck up 'The Teddy Bears' Picnic', whereat the girls filed smartly out of the room towards the Splasheries for one last washing of faces and hands before their first test of the day.

Walking down towards the lake that evening, surrounded by her chums, Joey had been reconciled to the idea of a swim. The exams had left her even inkier than usual, and a thorough scrubbing had done little to fade away the blue mess over her fingers. It would have to wait until she could charm some lemon juice out of Marie Pfeiffen, and there was little point in doing that until the end of the exams. She felt hot and sticky, and knew that her temper was beginning to fray a little.

Glancing over to the Seniors, she could see that Grizel was in a similar state, and was currently engaged in snapping at Rosalie Dene, who had ventured to disagree with her over the correct answer for one of the questions on the history paper. Shrugging, Joey turned back to Frieda, and agreed that the afternoon's English paper had been very hard.

'It was completely and utterly vile, and those were rotten sentences to have to parse.'

'Slang, Joey?' inquired Gisela, who rather unfortunately, from Joey's perspective, was sauntering by with Bernhilda. 'Pay a fine on your return to the school, please. You know the rules by now.'

'Sorry, Gisela. It just sort of slipped out.'

'That is as may be, but you still have to pay the fine, even though you have just made such a polite apology!' And, tucking her towel more firmly under her arm, the Head Girl continued onwards, vigorously discussing the possible questions for tomorrow's Scripture paper with Bernhilda.

Frieda took her friend's hand, and linked arms with her.

'But it *is* over now, and you do not need to think on it any more. Instead, we have the Tiern See before us, and we shall swim in it,' she said. 'We shall at least be cool for a while,' she finished feelingly.

'Yes. I do wish, though, that my sister had her camping licence. If only we could have spent the weekend camping out, sleeping outside, I'm sure we wouldn't be feeling so hot. I know for a fact I wouldn't,' replied Joey, mopping her brow. Even the short walk down to the School's bathing spot had left her feeling red in the face.

'But Joey, we have no tents!' replied Frieda, slightly wearily. The Middles had been vociferous in their desire to go camping, and Frieda was personally of the opinion that, since they couldn't do so, she would rather not discuss the idea at all, since all the talk in the world would not change that fact.

'And anyhow,' interjected Miss Maynard, coming up behind them, 'neither Miss Bettany nor I are qualified to take you camping yet. It says quite clearly at the back of the handbook that a Guider has to satisfy her Commissioner that she is fully qualified to do so, and, since our local Commissioner is in Germany, that will take slightly more organising than you would think.'

'Germany? Not Vienna?'

'No, Jo. Really, I think the exams must have addled your brain! We are the only British Guide company in Austria, so we share Germany's Commissioner. We explained that to you at one of the first meetings. The British Guides in Switzerland are in the same position. Get changed quickly, please. The sooner you are in the water, the longer you'll be able to spend in it, fish that you are!'

The girls were soon in the water, and enjoying the icy chill of the blue, spring-fed lake. The Chalet School's bathing spot was quite secluded, and set away from most of the springs that fed into the lake, but it was still chilly during the early months of the summer. By late August, the water would be more pleasant, but it would begin to chill again in mid-September when they returned to school.

The Juniors, under the watchful eyes of Miss Durrant and Matron, were splashing about in the shallows, while the Seniors were enjoying themselves by diving for stones further out in the water. The Middles had, with the help of Grizel in her capacity as Games Captain, organised themselves into a series of races. Joey in particular was enjoying herself immensely. A natural swimmer, she had only really been allowed to swim properly since they had lived abroad, as ill health had prevented her from visiting any swimming bath in England. After a year in the Tyrol, she was a strong, fast swimmer, and easily beat her confrères in their races, becoming *de facto* 'Champion of the Middle School'.

Emerging victorious at the end of her last race, she hauled herself up on to the boat landing, and sat panting gently in the sunlight. Madge looked at her with quiet, though evident, satisfaction. There was nothing in the healthy, bright-eyed child's aspect to suggest that any illness had ever plagued her. Not for the first time, she thanked God for the inspiration, and the lack of funds, that had caused her to open a school in Austria.

'Tired yet, Joey-baba?' she asked.

'Not at all, old thing. I feel as though I could do it all over again. It's a shame that we can't be tested for any of our First Class badge without the Second Class. We'd probably all pass the swimming test right now! Oh, well, I'm going to play with the Robin for a bit now. Cheerio!' and she dived off the landing, leaving a few ripples in the water before surfacing around ten yards away and heading towards the Robin and the rest of the Juniors, who were engaged in playing catch with an old tennis ball.

To their surprise, the entire school found that the break from work had done them all good, and they were far more able to tackle their papers the next day. The evening's tennis saw Margia winning plaudits for the Middles, and she even essayed a set with three of the Seniors, emerging, very creditably, on the winning side by four games to three before she had to leave in order to go to bed.

'It's all the piano practice,' she explained seriously to Simone and Suzanne Mercier, with whom she was sharing Mauve that term. 'It gives me the most enormously strong arm muscles. Not just from things like scales, more from the pieces, I think. Especially some of the Beethoven sonatas. Those require stamina as well as strength, they're so long and full of notes.'

The two French girls had nodded, and let her prattle on, not fully understanding exactly why Beethoven was so much worse in a sonata than, say, Mozart, who seemed to sprinkle his pieces liberally enough with notes.

The cricket too, was great fun. This was a more festive evening, since the entire school was free from exams and even the Juniors in Le Petit Chalet felt that the somewhat oppressive atmosphere that had percolated down to them had lifted. All the girls gave full vent to the pent-up feelings that had grown during the past three days, and cheered the players wildly. The entire school took part, divided loosely into quarters, using the Guide patrols and Brownie sixes as easy divisions. The Cornflowers and the Poppies shared the Fairies between them, delighting both Joey and the Robin, who were able to be on at the same time and watch all the other matches sitting next to each other, while the Swallows and the Cocks took the Elves. Even Grizel was forced to admit the success of the tournament, although it did not match her vision of a grand match between the School and an outside team—everyone played extremely well, and she could see that her regular practices had paid dividends.

'And after this, we've got the last Second Class tests, and your birthday, and the folk festival to look forward to,' sighed Joey happily to Madge, as they walked back towards the school buildings from the playing fields. 'How completely and utterly topping!'

And Madge, for once, was forced to agree.

Chapter XVII

... AND TESTS

JOEY looked at her Promise badge, considered giving it one last polish with her jumper cuff, and then thought better of it. Like the rest of the Chalet School's pupils, she had shoe-cleaning materials stored in a small box in her bureau, and she fished out her buffing cloth instead. She breathed on the badge, gave it a final rub, held it to catch the light and then pinned it on to her tie.

'You ready, Evvy?' she called to her fellow-Poppy. 'It's time!'

'Yup!' replied the young American, as she threw her cubicle curtains over the rail in order to let the dormitory air. 'Plumeau out, mattress humped—it's not a day to turn it, is it?'

'No, not until tomorrow.'

'Mattress humped, shoes shiny, and everything shipshape and Bristol fashion,' she finished.

'Wherever did you pick up *that* expression?'

'Dunno. Guess it sounds a bit funny coming from me, though?'

'Just a bit. Do I look tidy?'

Evadne surveyed her friend, and blinked. Joey did, indeed, look unusually tidy. The ink stains of the previous week had been eradicated with the help of lemon juice, and her hair shone from the brisk brushing she had given it moments ago. Her shoes were almost bright enough to reflect her face, and her uniform was in perfect order.

'Very tidy,' remarked Juliet as she walked briskly past, also in uniform. 'Hurry up, or you'll be late for *Frühstück*, and then it won't matter how tidy you are, you'll still be in trouble.' And with that remark, she left the dormitory to go downstairs, and the two Middles followed dutifully.

Frühstück was a calm affair, which was just as well. All the Middles and some of the Seniors were in a state of trepidation, as today's Guide meeting would be the occasion when they completed their final tests as Second Class Guides. Stéphanie was to rejoin the company at the meeting after breakfast—she was gradually recovering from the shock of her mother's death, and the authorities felt that it was better for her to take as full a part in school life as possible while she waited for the arrival of her father, than to sit and brood alone. She still looked pale, however, and the dark shadows under her eyes betrayed her inner anguish.

'After all,' Miss Bettany had remarked, as she discussed the matter with Mademoiselle, 'though she is not the only girl to have lost her mother, I think they were very close, so it hits her more than it would Grizel or Juliet. Still, Grizel was very close to her Grannie; perhaps that will help her to understand.'

'And that, *ma chérie*, would prove beneficial for the two girls,' Mademoiselle replied. 'Grizel was very much affected by the death of her *grand-mère*, and I believe she still misses her. Juliet, ah.' Here Mademoiselle shrugged in a Gallic manner. 'She, *la pauvre*, was less fortunate, as she did not feel that her mother loved her.'

'Exactly. Joey and the Robin will do their best, of course, but Joey was too young to know our mother.' Miss Bettany's face clouded a little, as she realised that her own memories of her mother were becoming increasingly shadowy: born in India, she and her twin brother, Dick, had been sent to school in the Hills as there was no possibility of schooling in the village in which their parents lived, and they had seen little of them as a result, as the school was too far away to allow coming home except during the long summer holidays. 'The Robin is very comforting, though: remember how she helped Grizel last term? Maybe Grizel will learn from that, and help Stéphanie.'

'Ah yes, *la petite* Robin is perhaps the best possible comfort.'

And so they had gone on to debate other matters.

*

'Margia—*Margia*! Evadne would like the honey. Please could you pass it to her?'

Margia started, and almost knocked over her bowl of milky coffee. It was the practice at the Chalet School to anticipate the wants of one's companions, and she had been remiss in not noticing that Evadne was not supplied. 'Sorry, Evvy. Sorry, Grizel.' She made haste to pass the honey to Evadne. 'I was trying to remember the "Ds"—the Dangers to Health.'

'Which can't you remember?'

'If I knew that, then I wouldn't be trying to remember!' Margia responded acerbically. 'Oh, I do wish I hadn't forgotten it! Won't anyone help me?'

Meanwhile, a table or so along, Mary Burnett was coaching the girls in Ambulance work: as part of her First Class tests, she needed to have taken them through the Health rules, and had done this during the course of several Guide meetings. Now she was hoping to be tested on her Ambulance Badge during the morning's meeting, while the younger Guides would need to know how to do simple First Aid.

'So, Frieda, if Suzanne started choking on her roll, what would you do?'

'Loosen her collar and bend her head back and make her swallow small bread pills and sip water. Sometimes it helps to hit her on the back.'

'Anything else?'

'Try to pull out what's stuck?'

'Very good. Suzanne, I hope you have recovered from your choking? Good. How would you get grit out of Bette's eye?'

'I should not let her rub the eye. I should try to get it out with some cardboard tweezers. I could bathe her eye with luke-warm weak tea. I could put olive oil into her eye, and bandage her eye, and take her to the doctor.'

'Well done! Bette, can you add anything?'

'If the grit were in the lower eyelid, I could brush it out with a handkerchief or paintbrush. If the upper, then I could pull the eyelid out, and push the lower eyelid up to clean using the eyelashes, or I could roll the eyelid up round a matchstick.'

'Do you think you might wriggle if someone tried to do that to you?' asked Mary. She looked round the table, and most of the girls nodded in agreement. 'So, how would you stop your patient from wriggling?' Sitting forward, with a smile on her face, she looked friendly and encouraging.

'By sitting her down and standing behind her, with her head resting on my front.'

'Excellent! Well done, Suzanne!'

Suzanne beamed with pride at this praise. She was beginning to feel vastly more confident that she would be able to pass this part of her Second Class test, and it was a very comforting thought.

The bell for silence rang at this point, and the entire school hushed itself, ready to listen to Miss Bettany. She stood up and surveyed her pupils, before bidding them tidy away quickly and assemble in the hall for their meeting, as there was much to do. Suiting action to word, staff and pupils quickly cleared away, taking their dishes to the hatch for Karen and her staff to deal with, and folding the tablecloths ready to put them away before the next meal. The room was soon clear, and the girls assembled in the hall.

Several weeks of Guide meetings had given the girls a great deal of practice. Standing up as straight as possible, they formed a perfect horseshoe in readiness for their Captain and Lieutenant. The Patrol Leaders stood slightly to the fore of their patrols, proudly displaying their staves with the small white flags bearing the patrol crest in cloth stitched to both sides. They all knew about the life history of their patrol emblems, although they had not yet had the opportunity to grow the flowers, as the Founder of Guiding suggests. Smart and still, they stood, waiting to be drilled and then inspected, as they began all their meetings.

A little nervously, Stéphanie stood next to Grizel, Patrol Leader of the Cornflowers. She felt sure that Grizel thought her recent absence had let the patrol down, as she was not yet a Tenderfoot. This was entirely understandable. She had started much later than the rest of the company, and had not had the opportunity to follow the same programme. Still, Stéphanie was keen to catch up and to make her Patrol Leader proud of her, although part of her wished that Grizel could be more like Juliet or Mary. She had heard Mary teaching the Tenderfoots and Second Class girls as part of her First Class tests, and had observed how she had taken to heart the instructions for training in the handbook: 'If you get impatient and short-tempered so will she. Be jolly with her. Don't try and teach her everything all at once.' Mary was very good at letting the less experienced Guides make their own mistakes and learn from them, while Grizel was far keener on showing them how things should be done, in an authoritative manner. She did try to be more patient than came naturally, but for Grizel this was a real struggle, and one which would continue for much of her life.

Drill and inspection over, the Guiders divided the girls up into groups according to the tests they needed to take. Matron had been invited to the meeting to examine the girls in both Ambulance work and Health and Hygiene, and she was soon engaged in questioning them, her head to one side as she listened carefully to their answers. She consulted the handbook before asking the next question:

'So, what are the Rules of Health?'

'There are six Rules of Health,' replied Simone. 'They are Fresh Air, Cleanliness, Food, Exercise, Clothing and Rest.'

'Good,' she continued. 'Now, tell me, how do you keep a house fresh, Frieda?'

'By keeping the windows open and waging war against mice. By keeping the drains clear and ensuring a good supply of water.'

'How do you ensure fresh air?'

'Opening windows, particularly in the stairwell,' replied Jo. 'Oh, and making sure that the air can get in as well as get out. Houses that are well aired and dry and sunny tend not to have cases of consumption.'

This was an important matter, as all the girls knew: they were well aware of the dangers of the terrible disease, both from the work beginning to be done by Dr Russell on the Sonnalpe, and also from the Chalet School's insistence on healthy living, fresh air and good nourishing food. It was hardly surprising, therefore, that all the girls had taken this part of the health rules to heart. They had all seen how the white man's scourge could carry off loved ones, as it had taken both the Robin's and Stéphanie's mothers.

'Well done. Och, I think you have all passed—so could you go to your Guiders, and you, Frieda, send over Mary and Rosalie for their Ambulance work, please?'

'Yes, Matron.'

Mindful that they were being tested, the girls were on their best behaviour. They departed to report to the Guiders, with Frieda peeling off to deliver her message to Mary and Rosalie, and then settled into their respective patrol corners to update the log books with their doings. Each log book was beginning to look quite beautiful. Heads together over the Cornflowers' book, Frieda and Stéphanie debated how best to show the day's work, and whether a picture might not be in order. Grizel came over, full of pride at having completed her Second Class, to inquire what they were doing.

'We would like to bring the log book up to date. I have been speaking about the legends of the crosses of the Union Jack,' explained Stéphanie, 'and I should like to paint in what I have learnt.'

'And I have been working on Health and Hygiene, and Ambulance Work. I could show pictures of the different exercises, and illustrate the rules with pictures of soap and clean water and open windows.'

'Perhaps we should appoint you joint secretaries for the patrol?' Grizel remarked, after listening to their plans. 'Those are very good ideas. How much more do you need to do before you finish your Tenderfoot, Stéphanie?'

'Only one clause, now. I am sorry Grizel, but I still cannot manage the knots. They are verr' hard.' In her consternation, she became noticeably French in her pronunciation.

'Perhaps I could help you again this afternoon?' offered Grizel. She was feeling pleased with herself, and this often translated into magnanimous gestures. 'We can make up knots for the Patrol Box, in two different shades of cord, and that will help you to make a useful article for the company ready for your Second Class, too.'

Stéphanie flushed with pleasure, and looked happier than she had done for several days. It seemed that Guides was doing its work on Grizel, and making her, for the time being, a nicer person.

Chapter XVIII

A Birthday Camp Fire

'Well, there's many more of us than last year, but I don't see why we shouldn't sing under Madame's window again.' Thus Juliet, when Joey approached her to ask for ideas over what the girls might sing as a 'dawn chorus' on Miss Bettany's birthday. 'What sort of thing were you thinking of, anyhow?' she asked, her dark eyes shining with enthusiasm.

'Something jolly that we all know,' replied Joey promptly. 'Even the babies. And something without a girl's name in it, either. Remember the hoo-hah last year when we chose "Who is Sylvia?"?'

'Ye-es,' mused Juliet, pulling her long thick plait over her shoulder and fiddling with the ends, 'but I think you could find a better description for the uproar than "hoo-hah".'

'Probably. How about hullabaloo?'

'Better, but not much. Do you want me to ask at the next prefects' meeting?'

'What, how to describe last year's discussion?'

'No, you idiot. More how we're going to decide what to sing, whether we'll choose from a short list, or all think of a song and take the most popular; and how we're going to assemble everyone to sing it, and so on. We're not all in the same chalet any more, let alone the same dormy!'

'You won't just decide everything for us?' queried Jo stubbornly.

'No, Joey. At least,' and Juliet smiled, 'not unless we find you're coming to blows about it. Then, I think, we might just have to step in, in order to preserve the peace, you see!'

Juliet was as good as her word, and presented Joey's request at the next meeting. There was only a week to go before the great day occurred, so, rather than ask the rest of the school for suggestions to vote upon, the prefects drew up a list of five or six favourite songs, and submitted it to the rest of the school for a vote.

The whole school was sworn to the strictest secrecy throughout the entire process, with the natural result that, especially amongst the Middles, outbursts of more or less successfully muffled giggles greeted Miss Bettany whenever she entered a room. Margia and Evadne were particular offenders in this respect, with Simone, surprisingly, not too far behind; the sensation of keeping such a pleasant secret was acute, and difficult to subdue. Miss Bettany, therefore, was not entirely unaware that something was brewing among her pupils. Remembering the lovely surprises that had greeted her the previous year, however, she quite correctly assumed that something similar was in the air, and did not trouble herself to investigate the admittedly suspicious behaviour of the Middles.

Between them, the girls settled on 'Green Broom', a charming folk song that Mr Denny had taught them and which they had been practising for the folk festival, to be followed by 'My Bonny Lass She Smileth', a more rollicking tune best appreciated once awake (and, it was to be hoped, an apt choice) before the girls were to disperse to allow Madge, Joey and the Robin to spend some time together before breakfast.

Accordingly, on the morning of her birthday Madge was awakened well before the rising bell by the sound of various thumps, giggles and rustles emanating from the direction of the dormitories—and over in Le Petit Chalet, Mademoiselle was enduring a similar experience. Madge lay back on her pillow and smiled to herself, recognising what lay before her. After about ten minutes, she heard the girls creep down the stairs, apparently under the impression that they were quiet as mice, since Gisela's 'Quiet, please! We do not wish to waken Madame before we begin to sing,' was clearly audible from across the landing.

'That would be a rude awakening indeed,' she thought to herself, as, having heard the last pair of feet shuffle down the stairs, she got up and put on her dressing gown. A swift glance in the mirror told her that her hair was at least tolerably tidy, and she crossed to the window just as Margia (who possessed that useful attribute, perfect pitch) sang 'loo, loo, loo' to start each part on the correct note. Madge leant out to hear the song:

> There was an old man and he lived in the West,
> And his trade was a-cutting of broom, green broom;
> He had but one son and his name it was John,
> And he lied abed till 'twas noon, bright noon,
> And he lied abed till 'twas noon.

Madge smiled and applauded as the last strains died away, and settled down to listen more comfortably to their second song, resting her elbows on the sill and her chin in her hands. Then, leaning slightly further out of the window, she spoke to the girls below her.

'Thank you for such a lovely awakening! It was far more melodious than any alarm clock could ever hope to be! I think, though, that before *Frühstück* you should all go and change into scrambling gear, rather than your Guide uniforms, since you have to go and collect the wood for tonight's camp fire before we can light it.'

A camp fire! The girls exchanged eager looks: this was the

first they had heard of a camp fire, and they were thrilled. Madge surveyed the girls before her, smiling inwardly at their almost tangible excitement.

'I shall explain everything properly after breakfast, when all the day girls are here. Off you go!' And she turned back into her own room in order to complete her toilette.

Minutes later, Joey, now clad in short skirt and cotton blouse, her legs encased in heavy-duty stockings, exploded into the room, closely followed by the Robin (albeit at a more sedate pace). The Bettanys held each other in great affection, and the two younger girls keenly felt the separation from 'Madame' necessitated by term-time constraints. The time they were able to spend together was all the sweeter for its brevity.

'Many happy returns, Madge!'

'Many happy returns, Tante Marguérite!' and the Robin tumbled into her brevet aunt's arms.

'Good morning! Thank you for such a lovely treat!' returned Madge, holding out an arm to draw Joey into her embrace.

'And we've got more for you!' cried Joey, proffering a neatly wrapped parcel. 'The Robin helped choose, and with the wrapping up, didn't you, *mein Bübchen*?'

'Yes,' replied the small girl. 'I *do* hope you like it. It's—'

'Ssssh!' interjected Joey. 'Let her open it first!'

Madge settled into the pretty armchair in the corner of the room, with Joey and the Robin sitting at her feet, and began to untie the ribbon that bound the white tissue. Gently unfolding the paper, she drew out a gaily painted vase, covered in the floral art so beloved of the Tyroleans.

'Joey! Robin! It's lovely! Thank you.'

'We bought it in Innsbruck last time we were there, in the same shop that your coffee service came from. D'you like it?'

'Oh yes! It's so cheerful and colourful.'

'And here's hoping you'll have some flowers to put in it,' continued Joey.

Madge did indeed have flowers to put in her new vase. In fact, the day girls of the Chalet School had plundered their parents' gardens so wholeheartedly that almost every available container in the Chalet had to be pressed into service to accommodate the blooms that crowded the table in the big Saal.

When she had accepted their flowers, and their gift of a framed view of the Tiern See from the Sonnalpe (a view that would become especially dear to her in later years), she announced the plans for the day.

'After last year's adventures, this year I felt I would like to spend my birthday rather closer to home; without the danger of spending the night on the mountain!'

The girls exchanged glances, and Margia muttered, 'Tell you later,' in lieu of launching into a full explanation of the night they had spend in a goat herd's hut on the Mondscheinspitze, for the benefit of those who had not been there.

'Last week, at Guides,' their Headmistress continued, 'I asked you to think what songs you might like to sing at a camp fire because, for this year's treat, we are going to hold the first English Guides' camp fire that the Tiern See has ever seen. I hope that there will be many more to follow it.'

Gisela stood up and spoke on behalf of the school as a whole.

'Thank you for having such a jolly idea. Three cheers for Madame! Hip! Hip!'

'Hurrah!'

There was no doubt as to the popularity of the plan. Every face was beaming.

'Wonder what we'll do for a Head Girl next year?' murmured Evadne to Margia, under cover of the applause. 'Gisela's been bully, hasn't she?'

'Oh, yes!' agreed Margia, who would have continued, but for a chilling glance from Juliet.

'You are all ready in scrambling gear, I see,' continued Miss Bettany, 'and this morning, at least, will be spent collecting wood. We shall want a great deal in order to build something large enough to keep the whole school warm! Herr Braun has arranged for a section of turf to be cut from the meadow and Miss Maynard and I will take it in turns to superintend the building of the fire.'

'Please, Madame, what about Guides?' asked Stéphanie, tentatively. She had only one clause to complete before she could be enrolled as a Guide, and she was anxious to achieve this blissful state before the end of term. She was not sure, as yet, whether she would continue at the school after the summer.

'There will be no official meeting today but, since some of you have only one clause of your Tenderfoot or Second Class tests still to do, the Lieutenant and I will be available to test you this afternoon while the remainder of the school is resting.'

'Oh, good!' returned Stéphanie, sitting down. Almost immediately she bobbed up again. 'Thank you!' she smiled.

'Then this evening, after *Abendessen*, we shall light the fire and have a sing song round it; and,' she continued, 'we shall cook dampers.'

The Patrol Leaders had already been primed with this information, since they were to be responsible for preparing the ingredients for their own patrols that afternoon, but it was news to the school at large, and the girls gave a happy sigh.

'Does anyone have any questions?' Miss Bettany finished.

Margia stood up quickly.

'Will the Brownies be allowed to cook dampers too?' she asked. Her younger sister Amy was, with the rest of Le Petit Chalet, a keen member of the school's Brownie Pack, and Margia knew she would be given very little peace, were she to make dampers during Madame's birthday celebration, but her sister be denied the opportunity.

'Yes, I'm hoping that each one of you will take it in turns to help the Brownies to make and cook their dampers, so that they don't feel left out in any way.'

'What are dampers?'

This was Bernhilda. Although both she and Frieda had read many Guide stories since the idea of a school company had first been suggested, they were both still somewhat unclear as to what a damper actually was.

'Dampers are spirals of dough wound round a peeled stick and cooked over a camp fire. When they're cooked, you pull them off the stick, and put honey or jam in the hole, and eat them,' replied Miss Maynard. 'They are one of the easiest foods to cook outdoors—although a Guide should be able to cook a proper dinner outside after a little practice.'

'Will there be *Blaubeeren* jam to eat with them?' asked Simone. *Blaubeeren* was a great favourite of hers and, although she loathed the hot work of collecting berries, the thought of the delicious jam made her keep going when otherwise she might well have given in.

'There will be all the same sorts of jam as you have for breakfast,' replied Miss Bettany, neatly forestalling a plethora of jam-related questions from the Middles. 'I think, now, that you should all go and start collecting wood, if that is the last question. You all know where you are and are not allowed to go. I put you on your honour to stay within those bounds.'

By the mid-afternoon, when the girls were accustomed to sit and rest in the shade with books and sewing, a sizeable camp fire had been built in the middle of the meadow, well away from the withe fence which surrounded the school and separated it from the dry pine forest.

'In this weather,' Miss Bettany had said, consulting Herr Braun, 'we cannot run the slightest risk of the fire spreading to the forest. It is so dry, it would be alight instantly.'

'Do not worry, *gnädiges Fräulein*. As long as the fire is well away from the Chalet and the forest, with plenty of bare earth between it and the grass, there should be no cause for concern. If you will permit me,' he continued, with typical Tyrolean courtesy, 'I shall superintend the removal of the turf and, perhaps, the construction of a small ditch? And a ring of stones. To contain the fire.'

'Yes, of course.'

Surveying the heap of wood in front of her, well primed with pine-needle 'punk' collected by the Brownies, Madge hoped that Herr Braun was right. She turned to Mary Burnett, who was attempting her Fire Brigade badge, and asked her what she thought. Mary considered.

'There is plenty of ground between the fire and the grass: to make it safer, we could soak this earth in water, and make sure that we have buckets of water to hand, as well as shovels to shift the damp earth on to the fire if it gets too large.'

Miss Bettany nodded, and asked Mary to find Eigen, the hired boy, and ask him if they could borrow some shovels in addition to the pails of water that would, of course, be arranged round the fire. Mary ran off to find one of the Tyrolean girls to aid her in her quest; although she spoke German well enough, she found it hard to understand Eigen's accent without a little help.

That evening, after a light *Abendessen* of cold chicken and iced lettuce, with raspberries to follow, the school assembled round the great heap of wood. Buckets full of water had been placed at regular intervals round the fire, and all the girls understood the importance of prompt action, were the fire to grow larger than desired.

A BIRTHDAY CAMP FIRE

'I think this is the most wonderful way to celebrate Madame's birthday,' murmured Simone.

'It could only be more wonderful if we were able to camp out tonight,' replied Wanda, a little wistfully.

'Oh yes! That would be *magnifique*!' agreed Simone, her smooth, dark head nodding eloquently. 'Why could not Madame have learnt how to camp at Easter? It would be truly superb to sleep outside!'

''Specially in this weather. It's so hot, sleeping indoors!' put in Jo. She knew that there simply had not been time for Madge to gain her camping licence over the Easter holidays, quite apart from the fact that her sister only had her Captain's licence now because she had been on a special course, and could not be supervised with her company as would normally be required.

'If only there was some breeze!' sighed Marie.

'But there isn't; which is a good thing with a fire going. And, since we can't camp out this year, I s'pose we ought to stop talking about it. But it would be so cooling if we could.' Joey felt that she should discourage this fruitless discussion, though in her heart, she sympathised.

'Do you think Madame will allow us to camp next year?' asked Simone, loth to drop such an interesting topic of conversation.

'Don't see why not,' replied Jo, although, with her sister's engagement in mind, she privately doubted that Madge herself would take them camping the next summer. 'Ssssh. The fire's lit now—'

The babble of chatter that had been running through the school gradually died down, and, enraptured by the sight of the flames licking up in front of them, the girls began to turn their attention to the enthralling process of manufacturing dampers. This turned out to be rather trickier than anticipated, and there were gasps of dismay as several dampers dropped off their sticks and into the fire before everyone had had her turn.

While the Cornflowers were concentrating on their dampers and helping the Pixies, Miss Maynard began to sing 'Friends of all the World', and the girls gradually joined in. Favourite song followed favourite song; not just Guide songs but many others learned in class, culminating in a thoughtful rendering of 'To Be a Pilgrim'.

The flickering flames cast ever-changing shadows on the Guides' faces, giving each one a mysterious air. The girls thoroughly enjoyed themselves toasting knobs of dough over the fire—although Cyrilla burnt her mouth in her haste to try her damper, causing her to have speedy recourse to the nearest water jug, and prompting Jo to wonder if she would be able to take part in the next day's folk festival. A lively rendering of 'La Normandie', Cyrilla making up in spirit and verve what she lacked in volume, promptly squashed this speculation.

Finally, as the dying embers of the fire deepened in colour to black, and the girls' faces faded into the darkness, the atmosphere of the evening quietened. The sun had set, and a feeling of serenity fell across the girls, and they chose the Robin's favourite song, 'The Red Sarafan', to end their festivities. Led by Joey's clear, choirboy-like voice, the echoes of the song, beloved by all the school now, drifted across the lake and, to those villagers who had listened to the 'concert' as they went about their evening chores, it signalled the end of the day.

In the silence that followed, the girls looked into the fire, huddling together not for warmth, but because they felt that they were sharing a special moment. Then Madge spoke, her clear, low voice holding music of its own.

'Think, girls, of the similarities between this fire and friendship. There are different parts to the fire just as there are different types of friendship. There are the dancing sparks—short lived, but very bright, and often noisy and vibrant while they last. Quickly rising, they dance and bewilder us, leaving nothing behind but an empty space in the darkness. Then there are all the flames—some big and strong, and some small and weak—so weak that the slightest breeze extinguishes them, the way some friendships are extinguished by the faintest breath of adversity. The smoke, too, is like a friendship—but the type that seems to have nothing wholesome about it, instead cloying and stifling the friends who are locked into it.

'The embers of our fire, I think, are like the best sort of friendships. They glow for a very long time and give out more warmth than any other part. They are intense, yet full of a beauty which is less obvious than that of the flickering flames. And a breeze, or even a good strong breath,' and here she blew into the fire, causing the embers to flare momentarily, 'which might extinguish a weaker flame, will make those embers glow more strongly and more brightly. The best friendships may grow through adversity.

'Think, then, what sort of friendships you have. What sort do you give? What sort do you value the most?'

The girls gazed into the embers, thinking quietly. Many of them knew that their friendships were less like the embers, and more like the smoke, or that they found themselves offering flames of friendship, or were attracted to dazzling sparks. Pondering, they resolved to try and be more like the embers of the fire; 'steady and dependable,' as Juliet later wrote to Grizel, 'unlike the sparks of the beginning of our friendship.'

Chapter XIX

The Folk Festival

The girls were spared, for once, that feeling of deflation that follows even, or perhaps especially, the best birthday parties. The prospect of the following day's folk festival prevented what Joey had christened 'the abandoned balloon feeling'. As they prepared for bed, they made full use of the abeyance of rules that existed on holidays such as Madame's birthday, and bobbed in and out of each other's cubicles, chattering like so many magpies about the day's events.

'The best part was Madame's talk,' an exasperated Juliet retorted when Evadne and Bianca once again threatened to erupt into a riot on the subject, turning Yellow into a bear pit. 'And if you want your friendship to have an iota of a chance of reaching the same stage as the embers of the fire, you'll hush up and think about that rather than caterwauling like a pair of Liverpudlian fishwives.'

Bianca paused in her altercation, asking, 'What is a Lizerpoodlian fishwife?' in such a quaint accent that Jo was hard pressed to stifle a giggle, while Rosalie's bed quivered gently as she shook in silent laughter.

'If I tell you, do you promise faithfully to quieten down and go to bed, and to sleep?'—for by now it was well after 'Lights Out'.

Bianca considered. She was really quite tired, and worn out with wrangling.

'Yes. If Evadne agrees.'

'Oh, I agree. For all that, I already know,' replied the young American. 'Go on, tell, Juliet! Don't be a mean.'

Juliet let the slang pass, not wishing to start any further debates at that late hour.

'A Liverpudlian fishwife,' she began, in her best 'definition' voice, 'is …' She paused, uncertain how exactly to proceed.

'… is the wife of a Liverpudlian fisherman, famed for her exceedingly raucous voice,' finished Jo, who had been on the receiving end of a similar epithet from Jack Maynard during her stay at Pretty Maids.

'And a Liverpudlian fisherman,' Juliet hastily broke in, before Bianca had a chance to ask of her own accord, 'is a fisherman who sails his boat from the English port of Liverpool. Now be quiet and go to sleep! It's nearly ten o'clock, and if any one of you makes the merest peep between now and the rising bell, I shall report you to Matron, who is bound to dose you with some exceedingly nasty medicine to help you sleep. Pipe down, do!'

This was no idle threat, and the girls knew it. Matron had dosed Margia, Evadne's bosom chum, and an ornament of Mauve, only the previous week when, in a fit of high sprits brought on by the end of exams, she had kept the entire dormitory awake for an hour through her inability to contain her delight at her newly regained freedom. The dose had consisted mainly of camomile tea, with a little hot milk. Combined, they had the desired soporific effect, but they left a bitter taste that Matron, usually so accommodating in these matters, had neglected to allow Margia to counter with a lump of barley sugar, kept in the medicine cupboard for this specific purpose. Not wanting to risk such an unpleasant experience (Margia had waxed lyrical upon the tisane's aftertaste with the result that all the Middles felt they had experienced it personally), the Yellows piped down and settled to sleep.

221

Jo, as was her wont, woke first the next morning. She checked her watch, shook it twice, and sighed deeply—she had overwound it the previous evening, and it showed the unlikely time of six minutes past one. She felt sure, however, that it must be nearly time to get up; and she and Evadne had a particular reason for wanting to be awake early that morning. Knowing how hard it was to rouse her friend, she slid out of bed and into her slippers to cross the room and wake the young Rip van Winkle, regardless of the hour.

She chose to employ the same method that her brother Dick had used to wake his chums at boarding school. Laying her hand against Evadne's face, she drew it firmly down. Nothing happened. Jo tried again, and still Evadne did not stir. A third attempt passed with similar results.

Smothering a yawn, Jo returned to her bed and picked up her water glass. It was full, but the water did not strike her as cold enough for her present purpose. She drained it swiftly (for if she met anyone in the corridor, she could thus say that she had gone to get a drink), and glided out of the dormitory towards the bathroom. There she replenished the glass with fresh, icy spring water from the tap, and stole back towards Yellow, unable to resist chuckling to herself.

Dipping her fingers in the glass, she flipped the water into Evadne's face, swiftly stifling that young lady's shriek of outrage, and the stream of American slang that followed, with her hand.

'What in tarnation's name made you pull a stunt like that, you nincompoop!' Evadne wound up, as Joey removed her hand. '*Why* didn't you wake me the way you said you would?' she hissed at a more reasonable volume, the sounds of a not-too-distant investigation by Juliet serving to temper her voice.

'I couldn't,' replied Joey laconically, placing the almost-full glass on the bureau. 'Anyone would think you'd pricked your finger on the same spindle as Sleeping Beauty. You didn't wake up.'

'Huh?' Evadne had not yet roused enough to be able to deal with anything that wasn't completely straightforward.

'I tried three times! You were still asleep, and looked set to remain that way for the next century. And I certainly wasn't going to *kiss* you awake!'

Juliet, entering the cubicle, raised a dark eyebrow quizzically.

'I should think not, either. Do you have any explanation for this appallingly selfish behaviour?' She glared at the pair. 'Or any explanation for your presence in Evadne's cubicle? Does either of you, in fact, have any idea what time it is?'

Evadne blinked.

'No-o,' she drawled.

'It is a quarter to five!' ejaculated Juliet, struggling to keep her voice down. 'You have woken the entire dormitory, if not the whole Chalet with your antics. What were you thinking of? *Were* you thinking?'

Before either girl could answer, the dormitory door opened, and Matron stepped in, almost vibrating with anger. Her bedroom was closest to the girls' dormitories, so that she might be 'on the spot' should any of them be taken ill. Generally a law-abiding group, they had not, so far, fully appreciated the fact that her nearness meant that she would be equally 'on the spot' should they indulge in any unlawful behaviour, such as a midnight feast.

'*If* I hear *one* more sound from this dormitory before the rising bell rings, none of you will be allowed to take part in the festival. None of you should be awake at this hour—and you all know that if you *are* awake, you may not even stir from your beds until six o'clock. Then, and only then, you may prop yourselves up with a cushion and read. There are still two hours before the bell is due to ring, and it will be a miracle if you haven't between you roused the entire house! It is perfectly obvious that none of you is ill. Go back to bed immediately and report yourselves to Madame straight after Prayers. I have no desire to listen to any explanations now. In the meantime, I put you all on your honour not to read, no matter how hard you find it to go back to sleep, until six.'

'I'm sorry, Matron,' interjected Joey hastily. 'It was my fault, really. I—'

But Matron was not listening. Her eyes were fixed on Evadne, whose cheeks were slightly wet, and a further investigation of the pillow revealed that this too was damp.

'Since your pillow is wet, Evadne, you may come with me to get a dry one from the san. Quickly now, come along! The rest of you, go back to bed.'

Thoroughly chastened, Evadne followed her out of the dormitory, and returned moments later with a dry pillow. She was determined to stay awake until the rising bell rang, and she lay there mentally rehearsing her song for the festival.

Evadne's choice of the Appalachian Nursery Rhymes had been inspired by several Saturday evenings spent listening to the wireless while her father did business in Chicago. Simone and Bernhilda had been persuaded to try their hands at fiddling for her, but she had been forced to abandon the idea of other appropriate instruments such as a banjo or mandolin. Keeping herself awake until such time as she would be allowed to get up and escape to an important appointment with the first lake steamer of the day, she repeated her rhymes to herself, and contemplated where she might include a yodel or a bird call, if only she could be sure of its success.

Three and a half hours later she slipped into her place in the Speisesaal just in time for grace, and with a smirk on her lips that caused Margia to turn toward her the moment they sat down, demanding:

'Did you get them?'

'Yup!'

'Do they fit?'

'No idea. Didn't have time. Had to stow 'em quick!' And with this, Evadne fell to eating the rolls that made up their breakfast, alongside the milky coffee. 'I could eat a horse.'

'Please don't gobble,' Bette remarked, before returning to her conversation with Rosalie.

*

It was a somewhat subdued duo that left Miss Bettany's study to attend the final rehearsal. Miss Bettany had been extremely dismayed that two Guides could behave in so thoughtless a manner.

'I am more than half inclined to forbid your taking part this afternoon,' she wound up. 'However, since this would also punish the rest of the school—well, how else could they perform some of the dances; they would have to be cut—I shall instead insist that you give up your free time in the last three days of term and report to Matron, offering her whatever help she may require. I believe she has several sheets that need turning "sides to middle".'

Joey and Evadne looked aghast. Neither was deft with her needle, the continental girls frequently despairing at their efforts, and the punishment meted out by Miss Bettany was appalling. Not only would they lose time with their friends just before the long summer holidays, but the time that they would have spent lazing around, or playing tennis if they felt particularly energetic, would now be spent in mending.

'Furthermore, I would like you to apologise to the rest of your dormitory tonight, and to Matron, for having woken them so early and so rudely. Finally, I would like you to learn Hamlet's speech "To be, or not to be", and recite it to me on Wednesday morning. You may go and join the rest of the school for Mr Denny's rehearsal now.'

And, dropping their curtsies in the traditional manner, they departed to the practice, Evadne muttering that the punishment was peculiarly unjust because she had only been woken by Joey, and had only reacted the way any sane, sleeping person would to a dousing with icy cold water. Joey glared at her before opening the door to the Hall, where 'Plato' was preparing to conduct the school in his own arrangement of 'My Bonny Lass She Smileth'.

'And pray,' he inquired, poised to begin, 'why are you so late, maidens?'

'We are sorry, Mr Denny,' replied Jo, suppressing the bubble of mirth that invariably rose when 'Plato' was at his most Elizabethan. 'Madame wished to see us.'

'Indeed! Prithee, join the other little maids, and we will recommence.' He pushed an errant lock of hair back into place, shook his shoulders convulsively, and nodded to Mademoiselle, who sat at the piano, poised to give the girls their note.

By the end of the half-hour, the girls felt entirely wrung out. Not one of the songs had been sung without some sort of hitch occurring, and Mr Denny had lost his temper over Rosalie's mangling of a particular passage in the lovely Tyrolean 'Lieber Tag', condemning her to miming the song, with a declaration that she 'wronged the celestial Euterpe' by her mistake. Poor Rosalie was almost in tears over this treatment, since only one note was incorrect. His long brown hair more tousled than ever, 'Plato' stalked from the room, muttering that the girls wasted the gift of the divine Apollo.

'Well,' remarked Juliet, 'I have never seen him in such a temper. Perhaps he too had a bad night.'

She gazed unthinkingly in the direction of Joey and Evadne as she spoke, and both bristled. Evadne would have taken the matter further, had it not been for Frieda's calming hand on her arm, and Margia's soothing voice reminding her that it simply wasn't worth the trouble that would surely result from rising to Juliet's jibe.

'I would not be surprised if he stops us in the middle of a song this afternoon,' replied Bernhilda. 'I am sure he is perfectly capable of such a feat.'

'And you sing this afternoon, Ros, old thing,' comforted Mary. 'You know that song as well as the rest of us; you've never been wrong before, and you're bound to be right this afternoon.'

'Do you think so?' asked Rosalie, her troubled blue eyes seeking reassurance from her cousin. 'Just suppose I get it wrong again?'

'You won't. Now, if we don't get a move on, we'll be late for Miss Durrant.'

Miss Durrant's rehearsal was considerably more peaceful than 'Plato's', the girls finding the familiar reminders not to dance on their toes or to bend their knees comforting. They retreated to *Mittagessen* agreeing that Renée Lecoutier's description of the mistress as 'a regular peacherino' was entirely apt. It was as well for Renée that no-one in authority had heard her say this, as it would not have been the first time that she had been severely rebuked for using this term!

Marie's meal of ham and potato salad, served with delicious fruit drinks, and with fresh fruit to follow, also proved soothing. At three o'clock, when the festival was to begin, the girls were happily wandering round the garden in twos and threes, chattering to their guests and feeling more themselves.

The concert, which took place in the same part of the grounds as the previous summer's garden party, opened with Henry VIII's ballad 'Pastime and Good Company', sung by the Seniors, followed by the Juniors' turn. The Robin stood proudly in the middle of the little group, and opened her favourite song by singing the first verse in Russian. The other verses were in English, translated by Captain Humphries. Next came the Middles with the first of two sets of Folk Dances—they presented 'Sellengers Round', with its elegant arming and siding figures, succeeded by 'Jenny Pluck Pears'.

There was warm applause from the audience, seated in rows on the lawn. A brief disturbance, as a latecomer arrived and took his place, preceded the next item on the agenda, a Breton fishergirls' dance performed by the French girls of the school. Although Simone, Renée, Stéphanie, Aurélie, Suzanne, Yvette and Honorine all came from different parts of France, they had been charmed by the rollicking dance, which mimicked the waves of the sea. The pauses in the action, designed to show off the tall lace hats favoured by the women of the region, had enchanted them, and they had chosen the dance in consultation with Miss Durrant. They all wore lace kerchiefs knotted round their heads in lieu of the hats, and presented a pretty picture. The newcomer in the audience smiled as he watched one performer in particular, before settling back to enjoy the rest of the programme.

The Italian girls next performed a brisk, energetic tarantella. They had added bright, flowing ribbons to their dresses, and attached them to the tambourines they played throughout the dance, leaping about with both precision and verve. They were followed by three more English folk songs, and then the French song 'Monsieur de Cramoisie', which the girls enjoyed chiefly due to its jolly chorus '*Ho! Ho! Monsieur!*'.

The Tyroleans came next with a somewhat tame Schuhplättler. (As Bernhilda had said, it was impossible for them to throw even the lightest member of the school, Gertrud Steinbrücke's little sister, upside-down on to her shoulders to dance, since there was no ceiling to be had. Throwing a man up, in the traditional Tyrolese style, seemed doubly impossible.) The two Eriksens sang a Norwegian song, accompanied by Margia on the piano; she had obtained the necessary music via her parents, currently residing in Bergen where her father was a representative for one of the big London papers. The Seniors performed two more English dances, 'Laudnum Bunches' and 'If All the World were Paper', accompanied during the latter's sung choruses by the Juniors. 'Lieber Tag' came next, and Rosalie finally felt able to breathe properly again, having got that particular note correct at the crucial moment.

Appearing on the stage area to perform her turn, Evadne caused a minor sensation. Her imagination had been fired by too many afternoons spent at the cinema with a particularly remiss nurse, and she had managed to persuade her indulgent father to obtain a pair of white 'cowboy' boots for her—the contents of the morning's mysterious package. The effect was certainly startling, although the vast majority of the audience did not understand her footwear. She wore a blue gingham neckerchief, which had been suggested by Miss Bettany as being typical of the Appalachian hills, and she looked somewhat flushed. Assembled behind her, rather more conventionally attired, were Simone and Bernhilda, fiddles at the ready.

Without any prompting, Evadne launched into a creditable performance of 'Go and Tell Aunt Nancy', a typical hill-billy song. Grizel groaned and wished heartily that she could stick her fingers in her ears, until Stéphanie nudged her when Bernhilda started developing the song's theme on her fiddle, adding harmonies below Evadne's melody—for Appalachian music is noted for its lower harmonies.

The audience responded enthusiastically to this impressive act, and Evadne's eyes sparkled with enjoyment. Encouraged by the applause, she chose to sing 'The Swapping Song' next, rather than any of the shorter songs she had practised. The twelve-verse epic had a particularly grating chorus, and Grizel shut her eyes, praying for the last 'to my wing wang waddle, to my Jack Straw saddle, to my John far faddle, to my long ways home'. The musicians played with verve, but it seemed an eternity before she was able to open her eyes again.

Evadne's turn was followed by a Mazurka performed by Cyrilla Maurús, clad in national costume, and the school then joined to sing a selection of nursery rhymes from all the countries represented, cleverly arranged into one long piece by Mr Denny. The entertainment ended with some of the lovely German Lieder.

During the performance of this last item, a smile spread slowly across Stéphanie's face until she was aglow with happiness, as she realised just who the latecomer to the concert was. *Capitaine de frégate* Pagnol had been directed towards the performance by Rosa, and had slipped into the last available seat just in time to watch his daughter. Almost before the applause for the last song died away, and before Miss Bettany had been able to thank their guests for attending, or explain that there would be a collection in aid of the poor of the parish, Stéphanie broke away from the rest of the school and, with a cry of 'Papa!', hurled herself into her father's arms.

Chapter XX

Celebrations

THE day after the folk festival was grey and misty, hiding the tops of the mountains round the School: the Mondscheinspitze, the Bärenbad, the Bärenkopf and the Tiernjoch were all shrouded from sight, as though nestled in Shetland shawls. The night before had seen Alpenglueh, where the grey limestone crags of the Alpengluehjoch and the other mountains that lined the western side of the Tiern See had flushed with the rosy reflections of the setting sun. Alpenglueh always brought bad weather: the previous year this had almost caused tragedy for the School, as Grizel had taken it into her head to attempt to climb the Tiernjoch, bringing bronchitis on herself, and a serious fever on Joey, who had gone after her. None of the girls who had been at the Chalet School at that time could quite forget the few days where Joey had been so ill: and as she gazed now at the beauty of the Alpenglueh, Joey Bettany shuddered inwardly at a sudden remembrance of that time.

It was the last day of term, and the majority of the school was busily packing up its final possessions. Their trunks were nearly full, and they would pack the last of their belongings into overnight bags early the next morning. Their packing done, Matron sent them out into the garden with instructions to rest quietly until it was time for *Mittagessen*, which would be followed by a special Guide meeting. The mists of the morning had lifted, and the day was becoming warm and stuffy.

'It is far too hot for you to run around or play tennis. Either take the large parasols and sit under them, or go and rest under the trees. Some of you will be starting very long journeys tomorrow, and you will be glad of a peaceful morning.' She laughed, and made 'shooing' gestures with her hands. 'No, Joey! I don't need any help at present. If I do, I'll ask one of the Seniors. You and Evadne have done more than enough in the past couple of days.'

Matron had had quite enough of Joey and Evadne's sewing during their punishment, and was only too happy to let Joey go and rest with her peers. Neither girl was handy with a needle, and they had managed to sew only one sheet each during the three days of their punishment. Still, the end of the those days had seen their stitches smaller and more even than they had been at the beginning, and this would stand them in good stead for the future.

The girls slipped out into the garden, and began to debate the pressing question of who would be the next Head Girl after Gisela left the school.

'Well, I sure hope it isn't Grizel,' remarked Evadne, settling herself more comfortably against the tree trunk.

'Oh, yes! Can you imagine how bossy she'd be? It's bad enough having her as Games,' Margia replied feelingly. 'Only yesterday she was demanding to know just why I wasn't on the courts! On the not-quite-last day of term too! What's she like as a PL, Paula?'

Paula von Rothenfels considered the question, knitting her dark brows as she thought. 'She can be—impatient. But she does know a great deal about Guides, and she is always ready to tell us and help us to learn.' Loyalty to her Patrol Leader made Paula more circumspect than she might otherwise have been. She would far rather have had Rosalie, Juliet or Gertrud as her Patrol Leader—what the other three lacked in glamour, for Grizel was a very pretty girl, they made up for in patience; a virtue which Grizel was still struggling to acquire, albeit with more success since the arrival of Stéphanie. 'Grizel has finished her Second Class badge and helped many of us, and we have all completed some tests. I think, though, that Juliet is nicer. She hasn't done as many of the tests herself, but she is less impatient when she teaches. Perhaps it will be Gertrud, as Head Girl?'

'You think so? I think Juliet's more likely,' retorted Joey, rolling over and taking a more active part in the conversation. 'She's nothing like as shy as Gisela was when she became Head Girl, and Gisela's been a wonderful Head Girl even so!'

'Juliet?' interrupted Margia. 'After the—that stunt she pulled with the film people?'

'Yes, Juliet,' Joey replied, leaping to the defence of her sister's ward. 'That was ages ago. I wish you'd just let it drop! She's become a lot more responsible since then—you know how good she's been to Amy!'

Joey spoke convincingly; she had spent more time with Juliet than the others, both because of the elder girl's unfortunate circumstances—Juliet's parents had attempted to abandon her at the Chalet School, before being killed in a car accident in Italy the previous year—and because she was in Juliet's patrol. 'The only reason she hasn't finished her Second Class is because she's been so busy helping us with ours!' This was incontrovertible; Juliet was the only Patrol Leader who was not yet a Second Class Guide, while the rest of her patrol had passed almost all, if not all their tests and were threatening to outstrip her. Margia was temporarily quashed.

'Perhaps Gertrud will be Head Girl,' volunteered Frieda. 'Or maybe Rosalie?'

'Rosalie would be good, but she's younger than Juliet, and that *counts*.' Joey was not inclined to let go of the concept of

Juliet as Head Girl, defending her argument with the tenacity of a British bulldog. 'The Head Girl at the High School was always one of the eldest. Besides, Rosalie's probably only going to be in the Fifth next year.'

'But she might be, er, removed?' suggested Simone, uncertain of the exact word.

'Get her remove,' Joey corrected, almost automatically. 'But she's not even a prefect yet.'

'Bette might be Head Girl. She will be in the Sixth Form, will she not?' Marie von Eschenau, whose sister Wanda was among the departing grandees, entered the conversation. 'But she, too, is younger than Juliet, so perhaps she will be Second Prefect, as Bernhilda has been this year.'

'Or Games.'

'No, Grizel will be Games!' And so the wrangling continued.

On the other side of the lawn, Grizel and Stéphanie were deep in conversation. Grizel secretly hoped to be Head Girl, but she was a good year younger than Juliet and knew, deep down, that she did not yet have the qualities that a Head Girl needed. Brooding slightly, she listened to her friend babbling, perceptibly happier since the advent of her father.

'And so, because Papa has to go back to sea one last time, I shall be here for at least another term! I shall live with my aunt in Lauterbach, and come across each day! Is it not topping?'

Grizel managed to smile at her friend; her enthusiasm was infectious.

'Yes, it's wonderful to hear that you're not leaving just yet! But I'd be careful about where you use the word "topping". It's slang, y'know, and a bad example to set the Middles and Juniors.'

'Yes. It is so *very* descriptive, though, like all your slang.'

'True. Now, tell me, where are you spending your hols? I'd like to write to you.'

Meanwhile, Bernhilda, Wanda and Gisela were taking one last turn round their school, before the bell rang for *Mittagessen*. Each lost in her own thoughts, they walked in silence. All three girls anticipated that they would return to their homes, rather than going on to the Varsity or entering employment, as some British girls might expect to do. Instead of continuing their formal education, they would learn the finer arts of home-making from their mothers, in preparation for wifehood and motherhood in the not too distant future. This they had been brought up to expect; their brothers might go and train for a profession, but not they. Already they had had more education than many of their peers, and they were pleased that their experience had included their year at the Chalet School.

The School assembled in Hall for *Mittagessen* in a rather more subdued fashion than was their custom. It was the first time that any of their number was to leave—and to have three favourites leave simultaneously was quite a blow. No-one was entirely sure how the school would manage without them. Simone, indeed, looked quite tearful at the mere prospect of their departure, and it had taken the combined efforts of Joey, Frieda and Marie the previous evening to convince her that all three would not disappear forever, and that it wasn't worth while crying.

'After all, Bernie's Frieda's sister, an' Wanda's Marie's!'

Simone looked blankly at Joey, who hastily recast her sentence in somewhat more intelligible French. 'And Gisela's sister Maria is part of Le Petit Chalet.'

'So Wanda and Bernhilda will come to visit us,' continued Frieda.

'And Gisela will visit Maria, too! They will come to all our plays and concerts. Of this, I am sure,' finished Marie.

'The point is,' Joey continued wearily, her patience beginning to wane as bedtime rapidly approached, 'tomorrow will not be the last time you ever see them. If you can manage not to cry, then we'll brush our hair together again before bedtime.' Simone regarded this as a great treat, and, making a big effort, managed to swallow back her sobs.

Mittagessen over, they repaired to their dormitories to change into their Guide uniforms for one last, additional, ceremonial Guide Meeting, as there were some presentations to make. By special invitation, *Capitaine de frégate* Pagnol was in attendance to see his daughter enrolled as a Guide.

Smartly dressed, their shoes and badges shining, the Guides of the 1st Tiern See company were arranged in their patrols promptly at fourteen o'clock. Their Captain and Lieutenant faced them, and, at a signal, they marched smartly into a horseshoe formation. The officers then marched from the base of the horseshoe to the gap at the top, turned and saluted smartly. Arrayed before them were the patrols in order: Honesty, Cock, Cornflower, Poppy and Swallow, with the Patrol Leaders carrying their patrol flags on their staffs. All that was missing was the Company Colour.

'Good afternoon, Guides!' Miss Bettany smiled. 'I am proud to see you all looking so smart. You have achieved a great deal this term, and, although the path has not been smooth for many of you, and there have been stumbles and setbacks along the way, I am proud to announce that the majority of you have passed your Second Class tests. First, though, we have one more Tenderfoot who is ready to make her promise. Grizel, as Patrol Leader of the Cornflowers, please bring Stéphanie forward.'

Trembling a little, with a quick glance at her father, who smiled encouragingly, Stéphanie allowed herself to be led forward by Grizel, who smartly saluted the Captain, and then stepped back.

'Stéphanie, do you know what your honour is?' asked Miss Bettany.

'Yes, Captain.' Stéphanie was well catechised. 'It means that I can be trusted to be truthful and honest.'

'Do you know the Guide Law?'

'Yes, Captain.'

'Can I trust you, on your honour, to do your duty to God and your Country? To help other people at all times? To obey the Guide Law?'

Stéphanie nodded. The whole company saluted smartly, and for the first time, heart bursting with pride, she was able to salute too. In a small clear voice, quiet, yet audible to all, she recited the Guide Promise.

Miss Bettany smiled. She had heard many Guide Promises made in the past term, but each was special to her, and each was unique.

'I trust you, on your honour, to keep this promise,' she said, bending forward to pin on the precious trefoil badge. 'You are now one of the great sisterhood of Guides.' She shook Stéphanie's left hand—for Guides always shake with the left hand, since that is the hand that is closest to the heart—and the girl then faced about and saluted her company, who returned the salute.

'To your patrol, quick march,' was the order, and Grizel and Stéphanie marched back to the Cornflowers.

'Second Class Honesties, quick march,' came the order from Miss Bettany, and the Honesty patrol, led by Gisela, marched smartly up to receive their Second Class badges. They were followed by the Cock patrol, then the Cornflowers, the Poppies and the Swallows. Slightly self-consciously fingering the cloth badges that would be sewn to their left sleeves that afternoon, the girls waited attentively for the next announcement.

'Mary Burnett, quick march,' Miss Bettany announced, and Mary marched smartly up to salute the Captain. She had been a Guide for two years in Taverton in England, and she had been a sturdy, sensible worker there. Arriving at the Chalet School, she had had very few tests to complete in order to achieve her First Class, and it was this badge that Miss Bettany was about to present.

'Mary,' she said, and her musical tones deepened, 'I am proud to announce that you are the very first Guide of the Chalet School to achieve her First Class award. I know that much of the work was done before you arrived here: and I shall be writing to your old Guide Captain to let her know how well you have continued with this. Well done!'

Mary saluted again, and marched back to her patrol.

'Finally, I have one last small, but important, ceremony to perform before we close our meeting. In England, during the holidays, Joey, the Robin and I helped a gentleman who fell ill on the train. He has sent us a short note.' And Miss Bettany began to read:

To the Captain of the 1st Tiern See Guides, Austria

I would like to thank you, and your young sister, for your prompt attentions on the train to Winchester last April. Were it not for the training that the Girl Guides receive, I doubt that I should have been discovered and aided ere we arrived at the train's final destination. As it was, I find myself extremely grateful that your sister recognised that I was unwell, and sought your help immediately, and that you provided me with care and succour in my hour of need. I am now convalescing, and it has taken some time to discover you in order to be able to thank you.

In view of the debt which I owe you, I have made inquiries of the local Guide Companies and at Foxlease, to discover what a new Guide company might possibly like to have. All were agreed that a Company Colour would be an excellent gift, and thus I am sending a flag for the 1st Tiern See Guides. In the course of my inquiries, I discovered that Girl Guides may not accept any reward for doing a Good Turn, so this flag is presented by way of encouragement to keep up the Good Work.

I remain,
>Yours faithfully,
>>S J Harris
>>Brigadier (retired)

Miss Bettany nodded to Miss Maynard, who walked to the corner of the room and brought forward a canvas case which had previously lain unobserved. The girls watched with interest as she unstrapped the fastening, and drew out a deep blue cotton flag with a green Guide trefoil surrounded by the motto on a red band, and headed '1st Tiern See Guides' in gold letters.

'Coo,' murmured Jo to Juliet, 'what a lovely thing for him to do. He was quite horrible when we first met him, too!'

Just as Juliet was about to motion her to be silent, she raised her voice.

'Three cheers for Brigadier Harris. Hip, hip—'

'Hurrah!' The Guides cheered with all their might. Although they knew full well that the flag was not what made the company—the girls themselves made that—even so, just as their uniforms had helped them to feel more Guide-like earlier in the term, so the flag made them feel more like a proper company.

Miss Bettany let them have their heads for a few moments, then motioned for quiet. Thoughtfully she surveyed her Guides, the Guides of the Chalet School, memories of the term's achievements crowding through her mind. At last she spoke.

'Next term, we shall have a dedication ceremony for the flag, so that it can be blessed, and so that we can carry it for Parades.'

She smiled round at them all.

'Company, dismiss!'

AFTERWORD

(All page numbers refer to Chambers hardback editions unless otherwise stated.)

Maintaining coherence within a writer's own world is hard enough: maintaining it within another writer's world is even harder, and there have been several moments where a decision had to be made that could do with further explanation.

STÉPHANIE AND AURÉLIE PAGNOL

Stéphanie is named in *Jo of the Chalet School*, *The Head Girl of the Chalet School* and *The Chalet School in Exile*. Initially she is mentioned as one of two new girls, a Senior, who had been at school in Vienna, but who came home because her mother was ill. Owing to the presence of an accent in her name, at least in the book in which she is first mentioned, Stéphanie in my mind had to have a French background, and thus became half French and half Austrian. This allowed me to let her grow up in the Midi, and also to give her a father who was away with the Navy—in the mid-1920s, Austria did not have a fleet to speak of, as it had been ceded to Italy after the First World War. Stéphanie reappears in *Head Girl* and is recorded as living in Lauterbach: so in my version of her story, she went after her mother's death to live with her maternal relatives. This means that, by the time of the Anschluss, she is still living in Austria and Joey Maynard is rightly worried about her whereabouts. Where her father is by this time is anyone's guess, as war has a tendency to split families.

I have taken the younger girl mentioned as being her cousin, and named her Aurélie after my French Exchange partner: physically, the two girls resemble the real-life Aurélie.

Stéphanie's surname, which EBD does not give, is in homage to the author Marcel Pagnol, whom I studied at A-Level, and whose writing gave me such a clear picture of the Midi and its thunderstorms.

Capitaine de Frégate Pagnol

The *capitaine*'s rank is equivalent to Commander in the Royal Navy: for a man of his length of service, one could reasonably assume that he might be a Captain proper; however, James Bond was a Commander in the RNVR and I do enjoy Ian Fleming's books. He needed a job that would keep him away from his family for a reasonably long period, and which would also make it hard to contact him. Since the Chalet School series already has absentee parents who are explorers and scientists, as well as Dick Bettany working in the Forestry in India, the Navy seemed an excellent alternative.

The Maynard Family and Pretty Maids

Joey Bettany's sojourn with the Robin at Pretty Maids while her sister is at Foxlease gives us the occasion both for the snail to crawl along the windows (as mentioned in *The Princess of the Chalet School*, p84), and for Joey to meet Jack Maynard for the first time.

By the time we encounter him at the Chalet School, Jack is well known to the Bettany family. It took a great deal of thought to work out exactly where in his medical career he is at this stage: reaching the end of his studies and about to move to work in a big London Hospital (possibly St Thomas's) seems most likely as he will later be an assistant on the Sonnalpe. Although further on in the series Jack is definitely Mollie Maynard's twin, at this stage their relationship is less defined. In fact, Jack has been described as her younger brother in the short story

'Joey's Convict' (p69 of the *Second Chalet Book for Girls*), and her eldest brother in *Head Girl* (p19). Later on, he is defined simply as being younger than Captain Bob Maynard in *Jo to the Rescue* (p141) as he inherits Pretty Maids after Bob's death, and finally in *The Chalet School Reunion* (p48) he becomes Mollie Maynard's twin—this is also stated in Chalet Club News Letter 12 (GGBP edition p53).

At this point in the series we don't yet know what Miss Maynard's first name is, so I have avoided its use where practicable. Mr Maynard is referred to as 'the Squire' in the short story 'Joey's Convict'.

It seemed highly plausible that Rolf would be the type of spoilt, selfish boy that would disturb two girls' sleep by planting snails on the window pane. Rolf is a year or so younger than Joey—in *The Chalet School Goes to It*, he 'would be nearly nineteen' (p11) if he had not died. How, exactly, Rolf dies is unclear; however, we know he was thirteen years old (*Rescue* p142) when he died in an unspecified accident which had been the result of disobedience that Lydia Maynard had never tried to control (*Shocks for the Chalet School* p29).

Skirting round the question of religion, Mollie is not Catholic at this stage of proceedings and, although Elinor states in the Chalet Club News Letters that Jack was a cradle Catholic, he is definitely Church of England in *The Rivals of the Chalet School* (pp215–6), as he attends a Protestant service in the Chalet School's own chapel along with many of the other English residents of the Sonnalpe. It seems more likely that he 'became' Catholic round about the same time as Elinor herself converted—doubtless she had forgotten that she had ever shown him as a Protestant. It would have been impossible for Mr and Mrs Maynard to have had a mixed marriage where half their children were Catholic and half were Protestant, as the religious mores of the time would have ensured that the children of such a marriage were brought up Catholic. Thus they go to the local church and we can assume that this is Church of England.

Guiding

By the time of the story, in 1926, Guiding has been in full swing in England for sixteen years, and in India for fifteen, which means that it is not inconceivable for Madge to have been a Girl Guide in India in an Anglo-Indian Company, during this period. Incidentally, in the early 20th Century an Anglo-Indian child was a British child born in India; see for example Vyvyen Brendon's definition in *Children of the Raj*. By the 1950s, when Rose Kerr refers to Anglo-Indian Girl Guides in *The Story of a Million Girls*, she means children of mixed race. The best information about Guiding in India is found on http://en.wikipedia.org/wiki/Bharat_Scouts_and_Guides. Information about the movement in Hungary given at http://en.wikipedia.org/wiki/Magyar_Cserkészlány_Szövetség refers to the Girl Guides of Hungary, but in Rose Kerr's Book they are referred to as Girl Scouts, so I have taken that description as being more of the period. In Austria, the movement didn't really get off the ground during the 1920s, but did better in the 1930s.

Although EBD gives the four Patrols of the Chalet School as Cornflower, Cock, Poppy and Swallow (*Princess* p114), there was not, in real life, a Cock Patrol. I have therefore adopted the shoulder knot of the Bantam Patrol for their colours, as suggested by the archivist at Girlguiding UK Commonwealth Headquarters. The Honesty Patrol is my own invention: as a Guide, I was a member of a 'Senior' Patrol as I finished my last year at Guides and worked towards my Baden-Powell Trefoil with two friends. I felt that for the eldest four girls of the school, there was little sense in starting a Ranger Company for the sake of a term's worth of Guiding, particularly considering that they have no experience of the movement other than what they've read in books.

Some have wondered whether EBD is incorrect in allowing both bird and flower patrols in the one company. In the 1919 handbook *Girl Guiding*, Baden-Powell states that it is up to each patrol to decide its badge when it is first formed; and although most companies had either bird patrols or flower patrols, there was no formal requirement for the company to do so.

Agnes Maynard deserves special mention: quite apart from sharing Miss Maynard's surname, she was pivotal in the development of the Girl Guides. Originally from Woodside, Wimbledon, she ran a training home for 'difficult girls' in the Merton area, and founded 1st Wimbledon Guides, one of the first Guide Companies, in 1910. Her signature is scattered throughout the logbooks at Foxlease, and she wrote the 1947 handbook *Be Prepared*. She is recorded in Rose Kerr's *The Story of the Girl Guides* as being 'a marvellous captain … her keenness and enthusiasm were infectious' (p53), and in 1936 she helped with the training of Austrian Guiders at the Archduchess Ileana's home, Sonnberg (Rose Kerr, *The Story of a Million Girls* pp229–233).

'Strawberry Hill' is a subtype of Georgian gothic architecture which takes its name from Horace Walpole's villa or 'little Gothic castle' of the name in Richmond. The style is also described as Georgian Rococo, and draws its inspiration from the tombs in Westminster Abbey and Canterbury Cathedral. The Strawberry Hill panels in Foxlease are thus very ornate and pointy.

Madge's treatment of the Brigadier's angina is taken from the section on 'Shock' in the 1928 edition of *Girl Guide Badges and How to Win Them*. The girls' discussions on how to remove grit from an eye are from the same source, and I would advise everyone to go on a more up-to-date First Aid course instead of relying on Ambulance advice from the 1920s! Incidentally, the Bettanys and the Brigadier are travelling in a 'composite corridor brake' carriage, with adjacent 1st and 3rd class compartments. The Brigadier is in the 1st class.

In 1929, Brownies wore a brown tie, which they had to be able to tie. The Brownie Uniform of 1914, which also includes a tie, is shown on the Norfolk Archive's web page http://www.girlguidingnorfolkheritage.org.uk/uniforms/index.php, and this leads me to believe that the Brownies of 1926 would wear one. At this period, Promise Badges were referred to as 'Tenderfoot badges' or 'badge brooches'.

The Guides of the Chalet School were well equipped to try for their Folk Song and Dance badge the moment they got their Second Class badges. In fact, by this point, they know the following dances in Cecil Sharp's list: Pop Goes the Weasel, If All the World Were Paper, Gallopede, Jenny Pluck Pears, The Butterfly/Butterflies, Uptails All, Gathering Peascods, Black Nag, Haste to the Wedding, Three Meet, Tink-a-Tink/Tink-a-Wink—and they only need to know four of these. The syllabus doesn't say that the folk songs also have to come from Cecil Sharp's collection.

Uniform

In *Princess* (p112) Elisaveta, making her promise, is described as wearing a 'blue jumper and skirt, with her yellow tie hanging loose'. Information culled from the publication 'Guiding Through Time', published by Girlguiding Scotland, and also from my 1929 edition of the *Official Handbook of Girl Guiding*, tells me that this jumper was not so much a jersey as a long overshirt, reaching well past the hip, worn outside the skirt and secured with a belt (from which one might hang one's penknife or whistle).

The same uniform would be worn by Ranger Guides, then simply called Rangers. On her right arm, a Guide would wear her proficiency or efficiency badges, and on her left arm, her First Class badge and badges relating to Ambulance work and nursing. The patrol badge was sewn to the left breast, with the company's nametape on the left shoulder, securing the shoulder knot beneath it. The whole was topped by a broad-brimmed, navy hat.

JOEY AND MADGE'S AUNTS

EBD tells us very little about Joey and Madge's aunts, and my view of them is largely based on the work Helen Barber did for *The Bettanys of Taverton High*. I was lucky enough to be considering the Aunts and their families at around the same time as Helen was writing, and we exchanged emails, reaching a consensus about various key characters. In the first two books in the series proper, the Aunts have definitely played a significant role in the Bettanys' lives—they have to be presented with Madge's plan to start a school as a *fait accompli* and they fuss over Joey's health. They have large families and small means, and they do not look after the Bettany family permanently. Helen has defined their relationships in true EBD style, with one being a great aunt and the other 'some sort of cousin'. It is therefore natural, as Madge's life becomes more focussed on the Tyrol after her engagement to Dr Russell that 'the Aunts' play a less important role in the series.

FOLK DANCING AND THE FOLK FESTIVAL

Like many readers of the Chalet School stories, I had been bemused that the girls were forbidden to bend their knees while folk dancing. This specific style of dancing, in which the dancer gives at the ankles rather than at the knees, was encouraged by Cecil Sharp (known to fans of Elsie J Oxenham's Abbey series as 'the Prophet'), who collected folk songs and folk dances in the late 19th and early 20th centuries. Another school of thought—that propounded by Mary Neal, who did a great deal of social work with the poor of Soho and Marylebone, and formed the *Espérance Club* in Cumberland Market at which the girls learnt morris dancing—allows knees to be bent! Miss Durrant, like the Abbey Girls, belongs to the former camp.

The folk festival is loosely described in *Princess*, p266, which tells us that the girls did not keep to one country, but showed a variety of dances, and sang folk songs from all the countries represented.

JULIAN OF NORWICH

Julian of Norwich (c1342–1416) was one of the greatest English mystics, and was the first female published author in the English language, when her book *Sixteen Revelations of Divine Love* was published in c1393. As a teenager in Norwich, I visited the church of St Julian, where she had her cell, on a geography field trip. Although I have not read all of her revelations, her assertion 'All shall be well, and all shall be well, and all manner of things shall be well' has been a source of great comfort to me.

SUNDRY MEMBERS OF THE SCHOOL

Honorine Drouin: An unnamed new girl arrives at some point in the terms covered by *Guides* and *Juliet of the Chalet School*. Since I like my characters to be named, she became, in my mind, Honorine Drouin. I had a Canadian penpal with the surname Drouin, while the phrase '*la petite Honorine*' had stuck in my mind from somewhere.

Kitty Burnett: As far as information given by EBD is concerned, Kitty could have joined the Chalet School either during *Guides* or during *Juliet*; however, since Caroline had her join at the beginning of the autumn term, she is not mentioned during *Guides*.

BOOKS MENTIONED
An Inland Voyage—Robert Louis Stevenson
As You Like It—William Shakespeare
Daddy-Long-Legs—Jean Webster
Girl Guide Badges and How to Win Them—Mrs Janson Potts
Girl Guiding—Sir Robert Baden-Powell
Nursery Songs from the Appalachian Mountains—Cecil J Sharp
Peg's Patrol—Mrs A C Osborn Hann
Pride and Prejudice—Jane Austen
The Jungle Book—Rudyard Kipling
The Railway Children—E Nesbit
The Wind in the Willows—Kenneth Grahame
Wuthering Heights—Emily Brontë

Jane Berry
2009

Girls Gone By Publishers

Girls Gone By Publishers republish some of the most popular children's fiction from the 20th century, concentrating on those titles which are most sought after and difficult to find on the second-hand market. Our aim is to make them available at affordable prices, and to make ownership possible not only for existing collectors but also for new collectors so that the books continue to survive. We also publish some new titles which fit into this genre.

Authors on the GGBP fiction list include Angela Brazil, Margaret Biggs, Elinor Brent-Dyer, Dorita Fairlie Bruce, Christine Chaundler, Gwendoline Courtney, Winifred Darch, Monica Edwards, Josephine Elder, Antonia Forest, Lorna Hill, Clare Mallory, Helen McClelland, Dorothea Moore, Violet Needham, Elsie Jeanette Oxenham, Malcolm Saville, Evelyn Smith and Geoffrey Trease.

We also have a growing range of non-fiction titles, either more general works about the genre or books about particular authors. Our non-fiction authors include Mary Cadogan, James Mackenzie, Brian Parks and Stella Waring and Sheila Ray. These are in a larger format than our fiction titles, and most of them are lavishly illustrated in colour as well as black and white.

For details of availability and when to order (please do not order books until they are actually listed) see our website—www.ggbp.co.uk—or write for a catalogue to Clarissa Cridland or Ann Mackie-Hunter, GGBP, 4 Rock Terrace, Coleford, Bath, BA3 5NF, UK.

FRIENDS OF THE CHALET SCHOOL

Founded 1989

— an international fans' society founded in 1989 to foster friendship between Chalet School fans all over the world

Join Friends of the Chalet School for
Quarterly Magazines over 70 pages long
A Lending Library of all Elinor Brent-Dyer's books
Le Petit Chalet (for those aged 13 and under)
Collectors' Corner Booklets
Dustwrapper and Illustration Booklets

For more information send an A5 SAE to
Ann Mackie-Hunter or Clarissa Cridland
4 Rock Terrace, Coleford, Bath, Somerset BA3 5NF, UK
e-mail focs@rockterrace.org
www.chaletschool.org.uk

You may also be interested in the New Chalet Club.
For further details send an SAE to
Rona Falconer, Membership Secretary,
The New Chalet Club, 18 Nuns Moor Crescent,
Newcastle upon Tyne, NE4 9BE